PERSPECTIVES IN MULTICULTURAL EDUCATION

Edited by
William E. Sims
Bernice Bass de Martínez

UNIVERSITY
PRESS OF
AMERICA

LANHAM • NEW YORK • LONDON

Copyright © 1981 by

University Press of America,™ Inc.

4720 Boston Way
Lanham, MD 20706

3 Henrietta Street
London WC2E 8LU England

Library of Congress Cataloging in Publication Data
Main entry under title:

Perspectives in multicultural education.

1. Minorities–Education–United States–Addresses,
essays, lectures. I. Sims, William E. II. Bass de Martinez,
Bernice.
LC3731.P47   371.97   81–40171
ISBN 0–8191–1687–4   AACR2
ISBN 0–8191–1688–2 (pbk.)

To our students,

    May they grow wise, compassionate, and
understanding.

                        William E. Sims
                        Bernice Bass de Martínez

ACKNOWLEDGMENTS

CONTRIBUTORS

(Staff)

Bass de Martínez, Bernice
    Department of Education, Colorado State
    University

Bruner, Howard D.
    Department of Education, Colorado State
    University

Estrada, Lawrence J.
    Director, Chicano Student Services Program
    Colorado State University

Hiatt, Dana S.
    Title IX Coordinator/Conciliation Officer,
    Office of Equal Opportunity, Colorado State
    University

Kerr, Vivian L.
    Director, Academic Advancement Center,
    Colorado State University

Sims, William E.
    Department of Education, Colorado State
    University

Vasquez, Melba J.
    Department of Psychology, Colorado State
    University

Wallace, George
    Department of Education, Colorado State
    University

CONTRIBUTORS

(Participants)

Allen, Barbara N.
   Teacher, West Middle School, Aurora Public
   Schools, Aurora, CO

Berry, Gleneth B.
   Mathematics Teacher, Adams City High School,
   Commerce City, CO

Bunch, Shirley A.
   Teacher, East Middle School, Aurora Public
   Schools, Aurora, CO

Draeger, Louise C.
   Teacher, Alsup Elementary School, Commerce
   City, CO

Lewis, Karen
   B/M Curriculum Specialist K-12, Mapleton
   Public Schools, Denver, CO

Morris, Lynn
   Teacher, Clayton School, Mapleton Public
   Schools, Denver, CO

Schmitz, Marjorie
   Teacher, Clayton School, Mapleton Public
   Schools, Denver, CO

PERSPECTIVES IN MULTICULTURAL EDUCATION

Table of Contents

PREFACE

This volume is the tangible result of an
Ethnic Heritage Studies Program project, "A Seminar in Multiethnic Relations," offered through
Colorado State University to inservice teachers
and other school personnel during the 1979-80
school year. The seminar was designed to improve
the teacher-learner environment for children in a
multiethnic school system. Inservice teachers
from three school districts in the Denver metropolitan area were invited to attend one of three
seminars offered during fall semester 1979, spring
semester 1980, and summer session 1980. The
seminars carried graduate credit from Colorado
State University.

The seminar was designed to change teachers'
behavior and attitudes toward students of different ethnic and cultural backgrounds. The term
"ethnic" as used in this document refers to those
native-born Americans such as Asian Americans,
Black Americans, Hispanics, and Native Americans,
as well as recent immigrants such as Southeast
Asians, migrant workers from Mexico, Cubans, and
Haitians. These are culturally different people
who find the public school system somewhat
unresponsive to their needs. These groups do not
fit the White, Anglo-Saxon, middle-class national
image.

One of the major themes in the Ethnic Heritage Studies Program is the emphasis on change
in education. Teachers who are White, Anglo-
Saxon, and middle-class are likely to have little
real knowledge about ethnic minorities; they can,
however, learn to appreciate and assign positive
values to ethnic or cultural differences such as
skin color, eye shape, hair texture, learning
patterns, or linguistic characteristics. These
differences, minor as they may seem to some
readers, have served as major roadblocks to a
truly equal education. These ethnic and cultural
differences are viewed by most middle-class

teachers as having no value. Because of their lack of awareness, these teachers tend to restrict the effective education of culturally different students; human interaction is not permitted to become multidirectional; and groups of students within the school do not share opportunities, privileges and facilities on an equal basis.

Multiethnic and multicultural education is the key to an open society, a place where people having a variety of cultural patterns and ethnic markings can live more abundant and fruitful lives.

INTRODUCTION

It has been twenty-six years since the Supreme Court of the United States ruled that the doctrine of "separate but equal" has no place in the field of public education. This country has awakened slowly from the nightmare of segregation to a new and different demand for a good education for its wide variety of students. Brown v. The Board of Education of Topeka, Kansas created a climate wherein the idea of cultural pluralism could emerge. Shortly after the Brown decision, a small group of articulate educators started the push for multiethnic and/or multicultural education in American schools. America has, indeed, moved with "deliberate speed" to equalize educational opportunities for the traditionally disenfranchised--the Blacks, Hispanics, Native Americans, Asian Americans, as well as the more recent immigrants.

A mandate from the National Council for Accreditation of Teacher Education (NCATE) in January, 1979, requires that preservice teachers should have knowledge of and experience with culturally and ethnically different students. NCATE's standards for judging the overall quality of an institution include attention to multicultural education. Those institutions that receive NCATE's accreditation in the eighties will have strong multicultural education components as part of their teacher education curricula.

As a result of this increased emphasis on multicultural education, a number of questions need to be asked. What constitutes a good multicultural education? What can make it easier for teachers to understand and relate positively to the culturally diverse learner? What should teachers know and experience to make them responsive to this complex challenge?

There is very little in the literature of

teacher education about multicultural education, especially for prospective and inservice teachers. Some has been written about culturally and ethnically different children and how difficult their public school adjustment was, but few writers have the interest, knowledge, and experience to prepare a book that will enhance the preparation of teachers for today's schools.

A basic assumption of this book is that the more teachers know about students and their ethnic cultural groups, the better they can modify their teaching behavior to meet the needs of these special children. The focus herein is to present in a nonthreatening way information that will help teachers assure that the time ethnically and culturally different children spend in public schools is as beneficial, rewarding, and exciting as it is to the dominant culture students.

Perspectives in Multicultural Education will provide a knowledge base for teachers who already have an understanding of their own culture and the effect it has made upon their individual lifestyles and personalities, because they are undoubtedly ready to increase their awareness with the study of historical, economic, cultural, and social aspects of the culturally different. This book will help teachers develop a supportive philosophy for multicultural education as they become more sensitive and aware of cultural diversity.

Perspectives in Multicultural Education contains four major sections written by people with expertise in multiethnic/multicultural education. In every sense of the word this book is a collaborative effort. All of the writers have worked in a variety of educational activities and share a mutual and empathetic understanding of the great need for teachers in the nation's

schools to learn about, as well as to understand
and respect, ethnic and cultural groups who are
different from their own.

                        William E. Sims
                        Bernice Bass de Martínez

PART I: FOUNDATIONS OF MULTICULTURAL EDUCATION

CHAPTER 1

HUMANIZING EDUCATION FOR CULTURALLY DIFFERENT
AND EXCEPTIONAL CHILDREN

William E. Sims

Teachers sometimes find it difficult to modify their attitudes toward culturally different
and exceptional children. This chapter will
identify the changes needed to create a humanistic teacher education program that is more
responsible to the needs of such students.

The term "culturally different" includes
native-born Americans such as American Indians,
Blacks, Hispanics, and Asian Americans, as well
as immigrants such as the southeast Asians and
migrant workers from Mexico.

The terms "exceptional" or "handicapped"
refer to those children for whom the presence of a
physical, psychological, cognitive, or social fact-
or makes difficult the realization of their needs
and full potential. (Suran and Rizzo 1979) One
does not have to look far to see that this definition includes the intellectually different, the
physically different, and the culturally different.

Humanistic education is concerned first with
the worth and dignity of each student. Humanistic educators are concerned with more than the
content of a textbook; they are also concerned
with personal outcomes. Mary Jensen (1973) states
clearly that humanistic education is:

A value commitment toward certain
educational goals. Whereas traditional
education is concerned with the mastery
of content, humanistic educators are
committed to the growth of the whole
individual. They are directly concerned

1

with programs that foster psychological growth, including affective and
motor, as well as growth in cognitive
domains. They are concerned with
individuals, their needs and interests,
and how they relate to themselves, to
others, and to society at large. In
short, humanistic education is concerned
with a reordering of educational priorities.

HISTORICAL PERSPECTIVE

Since America is a nation of immigrants,
people primarily from Western Europe, Western
European intellectual and emotional roots must
be examined to establish the reasons for the
widespread resistance to teaching the culturally
different and handicapped student in the mainstream of American public school education.
Western European people migrated to America with
three seminal ideas that have had great impact
on education. These ideas were: (1) A perception of the culturally and racially different as
inferior; (2) an intense emphasis on respect for
authority, obedience to family and loyalty to
God; and (3) a disposition to regard anything
short of perfection as unacceptable. These
three seminal ideas were combined with other
beliefs to form an American ethos that has perme-
ated every aspect of life in the United States.

RACIAL SUPERIORITY

The first seminal idea, the perception that
those who are culturally and racially different
are inferior, has probably been the strongest
and most damaging part of the American ethos. It
would be popular, but not intellectually honest,
to write that the early American settlers and
their descendants reserved their feelings of
superiority for members of visible minority
groups: Native Americans, Blacks, Mexican Americans, Chicanos, Chinese, Japanese, and Puerto

2

Ricans. This simply is not true. The English
settlers believed, and this belief became a
vital part of the dominant Anglo-Saxon culture,
that their race was prime; they believed there
were a few other races they could relate to,
and they believed there were many less desirable
races that should be avoided socially but
controlled politically, economically, and culturally. From the viewpoint of the English
colonist, newcomers in the Americas that were
different were a mixed blessing. On the one
hand, they were necessary for growth and development of the country; on the other hand, they were
foreigners with alien ways. (Kitano 1974)

Minority ethnic groups--Negroes, Indians,
and later in the period, Mexicans (these desig-
nations were used in Colonial times)--suffered
indignities that were also inflicted on the
Irish, Jewish, Poles, Italians, Hungarians, and
Slavs. But those groups with distinct ethnic
markings, such as darker skin pigmentation,
slanted eyes, and other physical signs, had
additional problems with which to contend. Not
only were they foreigners with strange languages
and customs, they were also racially different
and therefore were subjected to a harsher degree
of discrimination.

Schools during the Colonial period were
influenced by the prevailing moral and spiritual
values of the dominant Anglo-Saxon culture. As
a consequence, culturally different students who
were white dropped out of schools in great numbers, and for visible minority children, things
were worse. The children of free Negroes were
barred from public schools even though their
parents were required to pay school taxes; it
was strictly forbidden to teach slaves to read
or write or to give them pamphlets or books.
In early Colonial days, the Indian was ignored
in educational circles. Later in history, the
Native American attended Indian schools, and to
a limited extent, white schools. Conditions

3

were poor in both instances. All Mexicans, whether they were "pure" Spanish and landowners or "half-breed" laborers, were perceived as inferior by early white settlers. Before 1900 they were already a subordinated population, having lost titles to their land because they could not supply proof of ownership. (Kitano 1974)

From the early days when white settlers gained dominance over the West, segregation in the public schools was a common practice. It is interesting to note that the three minority groups that bore the brunt of educational discrimination in the early days of this country's existence, Blacks, Native Americans, and Mexican Americans, are still finding adjustment to the public schools difficult.

RESPECT, OBEDIENCE, AND LOYALTY

The second Western European seminal idea, respect for authority, obedience to family and loyalty to God, also had far-reaching implications for educators. The education of young people has been of paramount concern to Americans since the colonization period. Pilgrims brought with them to their new country both the best and the worst of European traditions. Speaking first to the worst: pilgrims would fondly say,"Children are to be seen and not heard"; or "spare the rod and spoil the child." Consequently, children were treated harshly and repressively by those in authority. Puritan forefathers, on the other hand, were also well acquainted with the work of Martin Luther, and it was his idea that the young should be educated by the city. This focus on education resulted in a Massachusetts law that required each town with 50 or more families to provide a teacher to instruct children in reading and writing, and each town of 100 or more households to establish a grammar school.

Respect for authority, obedience to family

and loyalty to God as a part of the American ethos worked very well in most areas of social endeavor. The family unit was a nucleus of early American civilization; the father's role was clearly defined. Family members paid deference to the father's authority, and it was expected that he would bear up best under the pressures of immigration. (Krickus 1976) The closely knit family unit was directly responsible for all family members. In this supportive framework they learned to deal with adversity and were taught accountability.

It was in the educational arena where the seminal idea stressing respect for authority, obedience to family, and loyalty to God proved faulty. Respect for authority created a climate that proved to be conducive to the authoritarian taskmaster teacher. Early American teachers, in their efforts to meet societal expectations, inflicted both mental and physical abuse on school children, and it was done with impunity. Discipline in colonial schools was in harmony with the Puritan theology that children were conceived in iniquity and born in sin; that they were possessed by the Devil and that only by the most severe beating could the Devil be persuaded to depart from them. Thus it was a moral obligation of parents and teachers to "beat the Devil out of children." The whipping post was a familiar item of furniture in colonial classrooms, and anyone passing a schoolhouse could hear constant wails of anguish from children. (Henderson 1979)

Although the whipping post is no longer a part of today's schools, many traditional teachers still run their classes in a Puritanical manner. Culturally different and exceptional children cannot survive in schools with uncaring authoritarian teachers who place great emphasis on a rigid curriculum, who teach for retention of facts, and who give little attention to feelings, human values, and attitudes. Contemporary

American education is having difficulties meeting
the educational needs of all students partly due
to the emerging conflict with the seminal idea
that has become such an integral part of the
American ethos: respect for authority, obedience
to family, and loyalty to God.

Present social conditions make it difficult,
if not impossible, for young people to blindly
accept and respect authority. The idea of family
obedience has undergone changes, and loyalty to
God is not as meaningful today for the young as
it was for their ancestors. There is widespread
distrust of those responsible for government,
and the completely stable family unit is becoming the exception rather than the rule. American
confidence in leaders is at a low level and
educators, both public school and post-secondary,
once highly respected, continue to fall from
public favor. Existing conditions in American
society exert great influence on the school
system and it would be unwise to expect the concept of respect for authority, tainted in most
public sectors, to remain pure in the academic
arena.

QUEST FOR PERFECTION

The third seminal idea, a disposition to
regard anything short of perfection as unacceptable, is a lofty ideal and is probably responsible for America's position as a world leader.
The Constitution of the United States reflected
this idea historically by stressing it in the
very first sentence: "We the people of the
United States, in order to form a more perfect
Union . . ." The story of American education
is the story of a search for perfection; education in America started with the idea of the
creation of a higher type of man, and education
still embodies the purpose of all human effort.
The educational system in America, in spite of
its shortcomings, is the greatest educational
endeavor ever put together in the history of

civilization.

The seminal idea of perfection has brought
to Americans great nobility of spirit, outstanding achievement in literature, art, and music.
America has a notable tradition of freedom of
speech and freedom to dissent. America, in its
dream of "a more perfect Union," has tried
different ways of doing things and has been willing to attempt things that no society as large
and diverse has attempted before. The idea of
early Americans to regard anything short of
perfection as unacceptable has produced very
positive American progress.

The idea of perfection, however, has had
its negative impact on public school education,
especially on teaching exceptional children. In
the early history of American education, those
children who were recognized as different or
strange, i.e., imperfect, were not wanted by
their families and were not accepted in the
public schools. Most of them were not sent to
school; a large number were hidden at home.
During this period exceptional children were
placed in human warehouses euphemistically called
residential centers. Parents would not insist
on public education because of the social stigma
attached to having a handicapped child. More
recently, laws such as Public Law 94-142, the
Education for All Handicapped Children Act
enacted in 1975, have determined that public
education is the right of all persons--regardless
of their personal differences.

In spite of the Public 94-142, many people
retain their negative attitudes toward the
exceptional child. There are school teachers,
administrators, and more than a few parents who
believe that separate schools for the handicapped
offer the best educational opportunities for
these special children. These separatists are
not clear on why they want to keep the handicapped and nonhandicapped separate; it is beneath

their level of awareness, but it can be traced
to America's obsession with perfection. These
educational separatists rarely stop to think
that exceptional children must learn from an
early age to live with "normal" children, and
"normal" children have to learn from an early
age how to live with those who are exceptional.

IMPLICATIONS FOR TEACHER EDUCATION

Fifteen years ago the President of the
United States offered the following words to
the 89th Congress:

> Every child must be encouraged
> to get as much education as he has
> the ability to take. We want this
> not only for the child's sake--but
> for the nation's sake. Nothing matters
> more to the future of our country; not
> our military preparedness, for armed
> might is worthless if we lack the brain-
> power to build a world of peace; not our
> productive economy, for we cannot sustain
> growth without trained manpower; not our
> democratic system of government, for
> freedom is fragile if citizens are
> ignorant. We must demand that our
> schools increase not only the quantity
> but the quality of America's education.
> For we recognize that nuclear age problems
> cannot be solved with horse-and-buggy
> learning. The three R's of our school
> system must be supported by the three
> T's--teachers who are superior, techniques
> of instruction that are modern, and
> thinking about education which places
> it first in all our plans and hopes.
> Specifically, four major tasks confront
> us: (1) to bring better education to
> millions of disadvantaged youth who need
> it most; (2) to put the best educational
> equipment and ideas and innovations
> within reach of all students; (3) to

advance the technology of teaching and
the training of teachers; and (4) to
provide incentives for those who wish
to learn at every stage along the road
to learning." (Keppel 1966)

Minimal progress can be measured for the
three more difficult educational tasks listed
in the President's 1965 message to Congress.
Incentives have been provided for those students
who wish to learn, but the nation has not been
spectacularly successful in its endeavor to
bring better education to millions of disadvantaged youth, nor has it been completely successful in placing the best educational equipment,
ideas, and innovations within reach of all
children. These tasks, however, are immense
undertakings and will always require additional
work.

One task among the four, however, should
have been possible to realize in a short time;
it was directed at higher education, and concerned higher education's teacher education product.
Teacher education was challenged to advance the
technology of teaching and training of teachers.
The challenge implied that teacher education
institutions should examine their programs and
procedures and make necessary changes to improve
teaching skills in a changing social and political climate. Although there are a few innovative
teacher education programs producing teachers
who are equipped to meet the needs of today's
diverse student population, most of higher education's teacher education programs, unfortunately are much the same as they were 15 years
ago, and the beginning teachers that leave these
institutions are carbon copies of those that
left in 1965 or 1955 or 1940. Everything in
America has changed but its teachers. Schools
and teachers were not meeting the needs of all
students a decade and a half ago; at that time,
one fifth grader in three never graduated from
high school, and a million students a year quit

school. The old teacher education methods and techniques are ineffective for the present and may prove disastrous for the future.

Teachers educated in traditional education departments by traditional teachers are uncomfortable, unhappy, and low-productive in classrooms where all children, including the culturally different and handicapped, are to be educated. Traditionally-educated teachers have completed the required courses, passed the scheduled examinations, received recommendations from their college professors, and are now certified to teach in the public schools. They make successful teachers in those schools where the teacher is accepted as a benign tyrant, sole judge of success and reinforcer of academic progress, one who remains distant from the students and will not hesitate to reward the academically talented with the knowledge that they will be the leaders of the future. They are less successful in those schools having diverse groups of students, many suffering from the adverse effects of poverty, prejudice, and ignorance. Teachers who have not had the benefit of an innovative teacher education program are usually unable to resolve cross-cultural conflicts and cannot work for a just and equitable relationship between students and teacher.

Teacher education programs must, if public school education is to meet the needs of students in the 1980's, prepare teachers for schools where all ethnic groups and classifications of students will be present, and where all services and facilities will be available on an equal basis to all students. New teachers must be taught that all students must have equal opportunity and that isolation is impossible in this interwoven, inter-related society.

It is time for critics of education to stop complaining about schools and teachers and to start identifying solutions. There are teacher education programs that work and that produce teachers successful at their craft. Ironically, most teacher educators, even the most traditional, are fully cognizant of the competencies required of teachers to meet present and future needs; they are not willing, however, to make the changes necessary to produce a more competent teacher. Traditional teacher educators are resisting change for two reasons: First, the traditional teacher educator is comfortable with the way s/he has always taught, and secondly, traditional teacher educators generally do not believe in egalitarianism.

TEACHER EDUCATION FOR THE EIGHTIES

In 1980, culturally different children are being defined by courts throughout the land as genuine persons with rights to equal protection under the law, and handicapped children are assured a free and appropriate education. The primary problem facing public school teachers in the 1980s is the increased responsibility to provide, in the least restrictive environment, an appropriate education to the extent of the student's capacity for all minority and handicapped children. In other words, education for the eighties should strive to preserve and enhance cultural pluralism. The decade of the eighties will see new emphasis for the entire educational system, but special attention will be given to multicultural and handicapped education. It is fairly easy to provide excellent education to relatively few children, particularly if they are students who already do well. When the schools try to educate all children, as we do in America, the job becomes far more difficult.

The new focus for teacher education must be on humanistic affective education. Teachers who are prepared by institutions that have changed from traditional to innovative programs will be concerned with the worth and dignity of

11

their students; they will know and understand special children and how they learn and develop. Innovative teacher education programs will provide academic and practical experiences that will acquaint the future teacher with character- istics of culturally different and exceptional children, so that they can respect their moti- vations and appreciate their feelings and thoughts. A better understanding of special children can only come from exposure to them and knowledge about them. Fear of the unknown is a human condition; it can be reduced and eventually erased by nonthreatening contact with and greater understanding of the feared object. When new teachers enter the classroom with confidence in their abilities to teach all types of children, they will enjoy better mental health because job related tension and stress will be reduced. A teacher education program to prepare teachers for the eighties must include both traditional and innovative learning experiences.

GENERAL STUDIES

The place to start to educate teachers for humanistic affective work is with the basic part of the teacher education program--general studies. The focus for general studies must undergo some subtle changes.

The general studies sequence of courses represents a university's attempt to give students a critical understanding of the princi- ples, standards and methods of thought in major sectors of human knowledge and their inter- relationships. The innovative emphasis, then, should be on the individual student becoming knowledgeable about his/her own culture, and the effect it has made upon his/her individual lifestyle and personality. In addition to the new emphasis, general studies courses should be used to explore historical backgrounds and cultural aspects of different ethnic groups.

12

There are several courses that can provide
a substantial knowledge base for teachers who
will work the major portion of their career in
the coming decades. They should select, as a
part of their general studies program, a course
in contemporary race-ethnic relations in order
to understand Blacks, Chicanos, Native Americans,
and Asian Americans as they relate to the dominant cultural group. A course in folklore will
enhance the understanding of preservice teachers.
Ethnic minorities have voices, and in folklore
these voices are most revealing as they speak
in many ways of many things. Studies in folklore include analytical techniques and perspectives that will assist teachers when working with
culturally different students. The legal history
of minorities is another essential body of
knowledge for future teachers. America is a
country made up of immigrants, held together
first by codes and statutes and later by a
Constitution. Lawyers were primarily responsible
for the system of government presently in existence. Teachers will have a better understanding
of American ethnic history, in reality American
history, if they are taught to comprehend the
acts, codes, contracts, resolutions, and laws
that directly affected ethnic minorities. It is
appropriate for all teacher education students
to complete a general studies program that will
equip them with knowledge and skills to enable
them to make a larger contribution to present
and future societies.

PROFESSIONAL EDUCATION

A basic assumption of this discussion is
that traditionally-educated teachers are
adequately educated in their academic discipline
and that they leave professional education with
a basic understanding of the development and
behavior of children. This understanding of
children, however, does not usually include
adequate experiences with culturally different
and exceptional children, and it does not

emphasize to future teachers that the intellect
of the culturally different and exceptional
child cannot be separated from their emotions.

The professional sequence should develop
in student teachers a supportive philosophy
for culturally different and exceptional
students. In the initial course of the professional sequence, components dealing with urban
education, ethnic minorities and exceptional
children should be included. The second course
of the professional education sequence should
include, in addition to the traditional material,
modules concerned with: cultural influences on
children, value bias in materials, cases of
group differences in intelligence, and strategies to improve the performance of culturally
different children. The third course should
have the following infusion: behavior disorders
for culturally different and exceptional
children, strategies for teaching the linguistically different, and a tutorial field experience
with culturally different and exceptional
children.

The professional semester should serve as
an important step in the continuing process
of accumulating knowledge, skills, and sensitivity needed to function effectively as a teacher
in the coming decades. Each course in the
professional semester should include a multicultural and exceptionality component. Student
teaching should provide a total-immersion
cultural experience in either a rural or urban
public school setting. The total-immersion
experience will serve to synthesize all of the
experiences gained by students in their college
days. They will learn to feel comfortable in
a family setting that is culturally different
from their own, and they will learn to move with
ease at cross-cultural activities including
plays, religious activities, and other social
events. The immersion experience will enable
students to assimilate some of the symbols of

14

another culture, and communication styles, values, and attitudes of the culturally different group will be easily understood. This experience will present an intellectual, practical, and social challenge by bringing student teachers into direct and repeated confrontation with the gaps and inadequacies in their knowledge and understanding of culturally different and exceptional people.

SUMMARY

There must be increased emphasis on new information, strategies, and experiences for preservice teachers. Teachers in preparation must be able to reach beyond what has normally been expected of them; the citizenry will not accept poor professional development in future teachers. Teacher education programs that will survive the eighties must produce capable, humanistic educators skilled in diagnosis and prescription and sensitive to the needs of "normal," culturally different, and exceptional children.

REFERENCES

Denver Post, as reported in an article, "Sperm Bank Unique: Only Nobel Winners Are Donors", March 1, 1980.

Greer, Colin. The Great School Legend. Basic Books, New York, NY, 1972.

Henderson, George. Introduction to American Education: A Human Relations Approach. University of Oklahoma Press, Norman, Oklahoma, 1978.

Jensen, Mary. "Humanistic Education: An Overview of Supporting Data." High School Journal, May 1973, p.56.

Keppel, Francis. The Necessary Revolution in American Education. Harper and Row, New York, NY, 1966.

Kitano, Harry H. L. Race Relations. Prentice-Hall, Englewood Cliffs, NJ, 1974.

Krickus, Richard. Pursuing the American Dream, Anchor Press/Doubleday, New York, NY, 1976.

Petersen, William. Japanese Americans, Random House, New York, NY, 1971.

Schmid, Calvin F. and Charles E. Noble. "Socio-economic Differentials Among Non-White Races." American Sociological Review, 1965.

Suran, Bernard G. and Joseph V. Rizzo. Special Children: An Integrative Approach. Scott, Foresman and Company, Dallas, TX, 1979.

Weintraug, Fredrick J. and Alan Abeson. "New Educational Policies for the Handicapped: The Quiet Revolution." Phi Delta Kappan, 1974.

CHAPTER 2

THE LAW AND MINORITIES IN THE UNITED STATES

FROM 1620 TO 1980

Dana S. Hiatt

Before getting into a detailed discussion
of law and all that has governed our nation for
the past 300 years, I have a word for you; the
word is "discrimination." Discrimination--
according to the basic Webster's dictionary
definition--is a positive word. It means
discernment, and the ability to distinguish
differences. All of us have areas in our lives
where we would like to be known as discriminat-
ing people. The problem with the word "discrimination" occurs when it takes on attitudes other
people give it; when its meaning reflects the
attitudes of the person or persons using it.
In law, words are all important. The law is
made up of words, and one has to be very careful
in using words and assigning meaning.

Until 1620 this country had no legislative
attitude regarding minorities. Prior to 1620,
people of color were coming to this country
as free men and women, owning land, building
homes, raising families, contributing to the
civilization of America. These people were on
a relatively equal footing with all other people,
not of color, coming to this country doing the
same thing. Because, if we speak frankly, in
the 1500s everyone coming to this country was
running from something and hopefully coming to
something better, something that they could
build, something that they could structure to
serve their needs, to establish a society in
which they could live comfortably, freely,
equally. But in 1620, something happened that
made it necessary to legislate attitudes.

The Virginia Colony decided, in 1620, that

17

people of color were different from the other
people coming to this country and that, since
people of color were different, they were to be
treated differently. They were to be looked
upon as less than those individuals who were
not of color coming to this country. They would
be restricted; they could not own land, be
educated, vote, or participate in their local or
territorial government. They became, not
second-class citizens, they became non-citizens.
They became non-persons. They became chattle-
property.

The first concepts of this legislation
started in the Virginia Colony because there
were numerous people of color there. It was
the first recorded evidence of legislation set
forth to control or to limit a group of people
in this country. Gradually, the concept of
divesting people of color of their rights
spread.

Looking chronologically at the history of
legislation, one can see that in the early years
individual minority groups were the subjects of
legislative action. It was not until the 20th
Century that the concept of dealing with the
visible minority groups as a whole rather than
dealing with them individually emerged.

PRE-CIVIL WAR LEGISLATION

There are probably as many opinions on
whether or not the North would have been a
great slave-owning area, as there are scholars
who write on the subject of slavery. All one
can really do is to use hindsight and to point
out an important difference between the two
areas of America at that time: the distinct
economic bases. The South was agricultural and
the crops were those lending themselves to the
use of large numbers of people. The North was
also agricultural but grew crops that could be
readily handled by smaller groups of people.

18

Thus, the need for great numbers of free laborers was not as prevalent in the North. The
North was deeply involved, however, in slave
trading and there were difficulties with the
slave trade and subsequent attempts to legislate
the elimination of it.

One of the few things that Americans in the
North and South agreed upon in the 1700s was the
question of whether or not there should be an
end to the slave trade. The South wanted the
slave trade to continue because they needed the
product of the slave labor. And the North
wanted the slave trade because they profited
from the mechanics of the slave trade itself:
the ship building, the commerce, and the sales
of the product. Therefore,in the early period
of this country, during the time of British
control, there was very little nation-wide
effort to speak to the concepts of slavery. It
was controlled, by and large, through legislation enacted by the individual colonies.

Since there were differences in the way
people of color were treated in the individual
colonies, the argument has been made that the
South had stringent restrictions on the actions
of slaves due to fear. It is very difficult,
however, to reconcile the concept of fear of
slaves with the picture, so often promulgated
by the South, of the slaves as docile, happy,
peaceful people, glad to be where they were,
doing what they were doing. If the slaves were
happy to be doing what they were doing, why
should the colonists have been afraid of them?
And if they weren't afraid of them, why would
they need to legislate so stringently (as was
done in the Virginia Colonies) that they could
not congregate in a church without supervision,
be taught to read, even move from one plantation
to the next?

THE CONSTITUTIONAL CONVENTION

The slaves were further dealt with at the Constitutional Convention in 1787. The South wanted everyone counted as part of the population. The North said only white men should be counted. The solution was to count each slave as three fifths of a man for the purpose of determining the tax base and the number of representatives each state should have in Congress. It is important to remember that even at this time there was recognition that slaves could serve other than purely agriculture purposes. Slaves were important, and the existence of slavery was being recognized and, to some extent, accepted. Most of the Constitutional language on slavery reflected this spirit of compromise. The decision on the slave trade itself was deferred until 1807 as it was decided to let the nation grow and progress and then to look at the issue of the slave trade in 20 years.

The language in the Constitution spoke only of those people who were in bondage to another persen for life since, of course, there were still indentured persons in the country. The Constitution did not speak to the issue of the free blacks in the United States. The slave issue was not dealt with in detail on a federal or national basis by the Constitutional Convention. It rested with individual states to deal with the concept of slavery, control of the slave population, elimination of slavery, or perpetuation of slavery. (The federal government then turned itself to dealing with the Native Americans as discussed in the next section.)

THE DRED SCOTT DECISION

In 1857 a monumental decision was made by the United States Supreme Court. The Dred Scott case, actually involving two cases (one in the

state court in Missouri and one in the federal
courts of the United States), is an extremely
complicated case legally. Dred Scott was a
slave belonging to an Army doctor stationed in
Missouri. The doctor was transferred to
Illinois, which was a free state, and Dred Scott
was taken by his master to Illinois where he
remained approximately two years. The doctor
was then transferred to an area of the Louisiana
Purchase that was north of the demarcation line
of the area of slavery. Dred Scott went with
his master and remained in the Louisiana
Purchase for a period of some months. When
the doctor was transferred back to the state
of Missouri, Dred Scott, his wife, and two
daughters were taken back or went back with the
Army doctor. The doctor subsequently died and
his wife remarried. Dred Scott first filed in
the courts of Missouri saying that because he
had lived for a time in an area that prohibited
slavery, he was now free. The state courts
of Missouri agreed and said that he was a free
man by virtue of the fact that he had lived in
those areas which prohibited slavery. There was
an appeal to the Supreme Court of Missouri and
the Supreme Court overruled the lower court
saying that Dred Scott was not free because he
had voluntarily returned to a slave state and
he did not gain the right of emancipation just
because he was taken to a free state by his
master. Because the Constitution requires the
parties in a federal lawsuit to be from different
states, Scott was sold to a man from New York
and the suit was filed in federal court.

The premise that has been put forth by
historians is that the abolitionists wanted
an issue. They wanted a decision from a federal
court concerning slavery, an interpretation of
the Constitution and its viewpoint of the status
of the slave. There are many well-known jurists
who have argued since the time of the Dred Scott
decision and argue to this day that the court
improperly heard the case in the first place.

They argue there was never an issue as to
Scott's status, that it was well understood,
that the whole case was created to gain some
sort of interpretation. Whether or not this is
true must be left to speculation, but it is
important to recognize that it was a step by
step process apparently organized to get a
specific Constitutional interpretation at a
specific time.

An interesting aspect of the Dred Scott
decision was its timing. The decision should
have been handed down in the spring of 1859,
but 1859 was an election year and the decision
was held over until after the election in
winter. The decision also was not to have been
written by the judge who finally wrote it. It
was originally to have been a very short,
concise opinion stating, in effect, that Dred
Scott was not a citizen, that he was still a
slave, and that,therefore,the decision of the
Missouri Supreme Court was upheld. It didn't
work out that way because the abolitionists
vowed to make it an issue through the dissenting
opinion. Thus, Justice Taney wrote the majority
opinion. Essentially, the law that came down
in Dred Scott was that at the time the Constitution was drawn up, slaves were not viewed as
citizens under the Constitution, therefore, a
slave could not be a citizen of a state and he
could not sue in court. Thus, the courts had
no jurisdiction to render any decision, because
one of the parties had no right to sue. Since
it is recognized that at the time of the
Constitution slaves were not viewed as citizens,
the decision, although we may not agree with it
morally, was logical and legitimate according
to the law on which it was based.

The decision is important not so much for
what was decided as for the dictum that was
included. (Dictum is not law. Dicta are state-
ments that may appear in judicial opinions,
which are not always necessary to the decision,

but which have the force of forming opinion).
The dictum of Justice Taney went beyond saying
that Dred Scott was not a citizen and said that
no black person could be a citizen or have any
rights whatsoever that any white man was bound
to recognize. In effect, it destroyed any
rights of any free black men in any areas of
this country. And it removed the protection of
the legal system from an entire group of Americans.

THE EMANCIPATION PROCLAMATION

There are many people who would say that
slavery was a small part of the issues giving
rise to the war between the states in 1860;
then there are those who would say that slavery
was the basic issue. The truth is most likely
in between. Slavery helped to coalesce the
issue of the states' rights versus strong
central government. And that was the major
issue of the Civil War. The supporters for a
strong central government, primarily in the
northern states, said that slavery was wrong
and should not be allowed to spread to the newer
areas of the country. The southern states said
that states' rights covered the issue of slavery,
and if a state chose to have slavery it was the
right of that state to do so.

The Emancipation Proclamation was an
executive order, but a group of jurists at the
time felt it was illegal. One of the problems
was that the Emancipation Proclamation freed
the slaves, but could slaves be free in states
when those states were not part of the United
States and were, instead, a part of the
Confederacy? The Confederate States had their
own president, their own constitution, and their
own army. The Confederacy did not recognize
the right of the U.S. Government to have anything to do with them, thus, the jurists felt
it was illegal for Lincoln to free slaves in
those states. Lincoln issued the Emancipation

Proclamation as a wartime necessity because
slaves gave aid to the enemy; whether their
assistance was voluntary or involuntary was
unknown at that time.

Ironically slaves in the border states--
Kentucky, Tennessee, and Maryland--were not
freed by the Emancipation Proclamation. The
Emancipation Proclamation freed slaves only in
those areas in rebellion against the government
of the United States of America. Lincoln,
through his Emancipation Proclamation, did not
address the slave issue in states that had
slaves but that had remained a part of the
Union. Some historians say this was a political move because the Union needed every man it
could get. If Lincoln had freed the slaves of
those border states, that for their own reasons
felt they should remain loyal to the Union, he
might have driven them into the ranks of the
Confederacy. Thus, the Emancipation Proclamation did not speak to the issue of slaves in
perhaps, the only areas that Lincoln had the
right to enforce it. The issue of slavery was
not addressed again until 1865 with the 13th
amendment.

PRE-CIVIL WAR LEGISLATION
CONCERNING NATIVE AMERICANS

During the 1500s when people were settling
this country from foreign lands, the Native
Americans were, of course, already living here.
This fact did not, however, protect them from
abuse as a minority group.

The British and the French first looked
upon the Native Americans as necessary allies
during the French and Indian War. This war was
fought between the French and the British to
determine which country would control the northern portion of the continent. The following
statement, however, was written several years
after the French and Indian War, and reflects

the viewpoint held by the British, and then later by the U.S. Government, concerning the Indians:

> The right to govern savages, having been based on the principal that discovering gave title, the term conqueror is not used in the Charter; as it could not with propriety be, in reference to a loose and straggling multitude not formed into a recognized society . . . (Price 1973)

Thus, all North American natives were deemed as savages by Great Britain and other Christian powers. One example of that loose, straggling group of savages (that was not necessary to recognize) was the Iroquois League, possibly one of the most advanced groups of people the world has ever known. The Iroquois had a system of law and regulation that served as protection for the tribes who made up the league. They even determined which tribes were responsible for protecting which boundaries for the entire league.

The British further took the viewpoint that all Indian tribes were dependent nations and that their individual members were aliens. This viewpoint carried through past the Revolutionary War and became the way in which the U.S. Government viewed them also. Because they were considered dependent nations, it was necessary for the federal government to conceptualize a way to deal with them.

Three approaches were eventually taken by the Federal Government in dealing with the Indians: Legislation was first based on the Constitution through the Commerce Clause; secondly, U.S. Supreme Court dicta which established the Guardian/Ward Relation; and thirdly, the concept of land ownership as determined, again, by the courts.

25

LEGISLATION BASED ON THE U.S. CONSTITUTION

THE CONSTITUTIONAL TREATY CLAUSE

The following four examples, out of the hundreds of treaties that were made, illustrate the progression of treaties and the changes that occurred from one to the next:

> In 1778 a treaty was made with the Delaware saying that when it came to punishing criminal offenders, each group would punish its own citizens.

> In 1785 a treaty with the Wyandotts gave the Wyandott's control over their land. The government was not to interfere in anything that happened on Wyandott land as long as it involved people who were living on the Wyandott land, whether they were Indian or White.

> That same year a treaty was made with the Cherokees stating that an Indian who committed an offense against a United States citizen would be dealt with by the United States.

> Seven years after the government said to the Delaware, "you take care of the Indians and we'll take care of the White," it said to the Cherokees, "you take care of the Indians if they do anything to Indians, but if they do anything to Whites, we'll take care of them."

> In 1804 the Sac and Fox treaty said the Sac and Fox must turn over any non-Indian offenders.

There were Indians privy to the decision making process. They were few and far between, however, not because they weren't capable but

26

because they weren't wanted. A number of these treaties were made on the basis of the power of the federal government and the perceived weakness of the Indian tribe. Treaties were also made on the basis of the political party or the political viewpoint involved.

As treaties were signed with the Indian nations, America continued growing, thereby, surrounding and making isolated pockets of Native Americans. The question of removal arose. The removal of Indian tribes from land east of the Mississippi primarily was used as an answer to the growing problem of whether or not states or the federal government controlled and regulated tribes within their borders. Although at that time removal seemed a solution, it turned out not to be. The westward expansion continued along with removal until eventually the concept of the reservation was developed.

THE CONSTITUTIONAL COMMERCE CLAUSE

The Commerce Clause of the Constitution was used to control all aspects of trade with foreign nations; since the Indian tribes were viewed as foreign nations, application of the Commerce Clause was deemed appropriate. This clause, along with the treaty power of the federal government, was the constitutional basis for dealing with Native Americans.

The first recorded exercise of congress, concerning the Native Americans, was the Indian Trade and Intercourse Act 1790. This legislation sought to extend federal criminal jurisdiction over Indian lands, first in 1790 and again in 1832. Initially, the Act of 1790 established the following ways for dealing with criminal violations that occurred on Indian lands: if the violation was by an Indian against another Indian, then the federal mechanism would deal with the punishment; if the violation was by a white against an Indian,

then the mechanism was to be between tribal
representatives and white representatives from
the state or territory in which the Indian
land lay; if the violation was by an Indian
against a White, but occurred on Indian land,
then it would be handled by the laws of the
state or territory. The Act of 1790 also
required anyone trading with the Indians to be
licensed by the federal government, another
utilization of the Commerce Clause.

Several court cases arose later to coalesce
the manner in which Native Americans were dealt
with by federal and state government.

THE GUARDIAN/WARD RELATION

One of the first such cases was <u>Cherokee
Nations v. Georgia</u> in 1831. The opinion was
written by Supreme Court Justice John Marshall.
This case is important, not so much for the
issue of whether or not a state has the right
to legislate or govern Indian lands within its
boundary, but because of the statement of
dictum by John Marshall that established the
Guardian/Ward Relation.

Basically, Marshall said that the Indian
tribes held a position of weakness vis-a-vis
the federal government. Therefore, according to
Marshall, it was up to the federal government
to protect them as they attempted to cope with
the problems of dealing with a civilized
republic. Furthermore, since these Indian
nations were dependent and weak, the federal
government had the right to do certain things
even beyond those things that fell within the
realm of regulating commerce. The Guardian/Ward
Theory was used to justify the restraint on the
transfer of land by Indians and the establishment of criminal law that could, perhaps, even
take precedence over federal law. The treaty
concept in the Constitution and the Commerce
Clause had not attempted to deal with quarrels

between Indians; that had been left to the tribes to regulate. With Marshall's dictum in Cherokee Nations, however, steps were taken so that crimes among the Indians would be regulated outside the tribe.

Although this appeared to be a victory for the Cherokee Nations, some of the language suggested that the Cherokees were not a nation because its boundaries were contained within the boundaries of the United States. This case was another manifestation of the controversy over the concept of state's rights versus a strong central government.

THE CONCEPT OF LAND OWNERSHIP

The third approach for dealing with Native Americans concerned the concept of ownership. This doctrine again originated in a court case: Johnson and Grahams Leasee v. MacIntosh in 1823. This decision held that title to all land in the continental United States, which was neither a state nor a territory of the United States, was vested in the United States because of the colonists who had landed there. According to this court decision, the Native Americans had only the right to occupy the land. The government was saying, in effect, that simply because certain people had landed on the Atlantic seaboard, they therefore owned it all.

This 1823 case began over certain Indian lands that were being leased. The federal government stepped in and said the Indians did not have the right to own land; they merely had the right of occupancy.

This statement opened the way for later contracts and actions of removal. Prior to this time, persons could appropriate Indian land only if they paid a fair price and only if the Indians were willing to sell it; this implied Indian ownership. The court decision, however,

changed people's perceptions: obviously the
Indians did not own the land, and it was not
necessary to pay a fair price for it or for the
Indians to be willing to give it up.

The Indians never said they owned their
land, the colonists said they did. Land ownership was completely foreign to the Indians, it
was a European concept transplanted here. The
clarification of ownership became necessary
because, as the number of states increased,
pockets of Indian nations and tribes were
created. It was the viewpoint of state and
federal governments that it was impossible to
have isolated pockets with different laws,
different regulations, and different enforce-
ments. Thus, one could almost say the concept
of ownership was created for the purpose of
reorganization.

CONFLICTING LEGISLATION

The issue which governed was always a
concern because there were conflicting laws,
court cases, and treaties. The court case held
that Indians did not own the land while a treaty
granted certain lands to the Indians because
they had been removed from others, and the law
said the federal government had the right to
regulate commerce and that Indian tribes had
no right to enter into treaties with other
nations under the federal government. Another
consideration, the Commerce Clause of the
Constitution, raised the question of whether
Indian contracts were with a foreign country or
with a citizen of the United States. The
biggest problem with all these conflicting rules
was that they made it impossible for people to
sit down together and work toward common solutions.

The laws, treaties, and court cases that
dealt with minorities and formed the basis for
action that was taken were primarily economic in

nature. Does it seem strange to think of
economics as the factor in determining the
value of a human being? When you look at a
legal history of minorities, you look at a
process of laws and interpretations by courts,
judges, and juries, all of which systematically
moved to denigrate the minority groups' work
and value as people.

PRE-CIVIL WAR LEGISLATION CONCERNING HISPANICS

During the 1840s the law began to deal with
the Southwest and with the Mexicans living
there. The areas that are now Texas, New Mexico,
Arizona, and California were a part of Mexico,
but they were in some ways viewed as territories
by the government in Mexico City. They were
valuable but distant territories that were very
difficult to patrol, control, and regulate.

By 1844 this large area, particularly the
territory of Texas, had begun to see itself as
autonomous insofar as the government of Mexico
City was concerned. The Anglos in Texas had
increased from several hundred to 25,000 and
they readily outnumbered the Mexicans living in
that territory. The Anglo took the viewpoint
that, were they to be a part of any country, it
should be the United States. Mexico took the
viewpoint, of course, that the area was part of
Mexico. In 1844 the government of Mexico, in an
attempt to alienate Texas from its growing
association with the United States, did something
that the United States would not do for another
20 years: it abolished slavery. Contrary to
what Mexico had hoped, the abolition of slavery
actually threw Texas more toward the United
States because so many of the Texans had migrated
from the South and were slave owners. These
people viewed it as economically impossible for
them to lose their slaves.

In 1845, Texas was annexed to the United
States. And in 1846, the United States went to

31

war with Mexico. Following two years of fighting, the Treaty of Guadalupe Hidalgo was signed
in 1848. This treaty granted American citizenship to all Mexicans living in the territory
ceded by Mexico to the United States, which
included Texas, New Mexico, Arizona, and
California.

The interesting thing to remember is that
people of Spanish descent living in the area
become, if they wished to, United States citizens
although the rights and privileges that were
supposed to be enjoyed by all citizens of the
United States were limited in many ways when
applied to the Mexican Americans.

PRE-CIVIL WAR LEGISLATION
CONCERNING ASIAN AMERICANS

The 1850s marked the first general immigration of the Chinese to the west coast. With
that immigration came legislation to control or
protect, depending on your viewpoint. Most of
the legislation during this period concerning
the Chinese was state (California) legislation
rather than federal action as was the case with
the slaves, Indians, and Mexican Americans.

The first action to address the Chinese in
the state of California was the Tingley Bill
which attempted to allow the enforcement of
prior Chinese labor commitments through the
courts regarding the two ways Chinese came to
California. The first way was the coolie
process, which meant the Chinese were little
better than slaves. As coolies, they were
brought to California solely for the labor they
could furnish either to the municipalities or
to the mines. The second way the Chinese
entered California was with the credit ticket.
Under the credit ticket concept, six Chinese
companies bought passage on ships coming to
California and then sold tickets at highly
inflated prices to the Chinese who promised to

32

pay back the cost. The credit ticket was similar to indenture except the buyers were not
required to work for the company that paid for
the passage. The ticket holders could get
employment wherever and however they could
find it, but they were required to pay back the
passage money. Tingley a California Legislator,
felt that the Chinese were coming into California under commitments to perform labor and then
disappearing, and there was no way to enforce
the labor contracts against the Chinese. He
attempted to make a contract that would be
recognized and enforced by the courts. The
Tingley Bill was not enacted because at that
time it was viewed as unconstitutional to
enforce work contracts when the person who had
made the contracts was not given any prior compen-
sation for them; it was not viewed in the same
light as indenture.

People v. Hall

In 1854 in People v. Hall, the California
Supreme Court (five years before Dred Scott)
based its decision on a California law which
prohibited Blacks, Mulattos, and Indians from
testifying in court. The California Supreme
Court, in an interesting display of logic,
determined that the Chinese should not testify
in court either. The court's logic went like
this: Since Indians could not testify, and
since Asia was at one time the Indies, then
people from Asia were Indians and, therefore,
could not testify. In effect, the California
Supreme Court said the same thing of the Chinese
that the United States Supreme Court later said
about the slaves--that the Chinese were not and
could never be citizens and, therefore, had
none of the rights and privileges that citizens
are allowed to expect. We thus have a state
court and a federal court, within a period of
five years, coming to the same conclusion about
two distinctly different minorities, i.e., that
they are not and could not possibly be citizens

and, therefore, have no rights that have to be recognized by the majority of society.

SUMMARY

At the onset of the Civil War the situation of the four identifiable ethnic minorities present in the United States was deplorable. The slaves had been determined by law and judicial interpretation to be nonpeople with no rights that the majority of society was bound to recognize. The Native Americans, through numerous treaties and various court decisions, had been largely removed from their native land to other areas of the country as the economy, according to the concept of "Manifest Destiny", made it imperative that the United States expand. The Mexicans in the Southwest were apparently citizens of the United States and apparently entitled to the rights of citizens of the United States, but they had to deal with unfamiliar Anglo-Saxon courts to attempt to protect their rights. The Chinese were beginning to enter California in increasing numbers and were, therefore, seeing the imposition of laws designed to control their actions and mobility.

POST-CIVIL WAR LEGISLATION

Constitutional Amendments

In 1865 the 13th Amendment was added to the Constitution of the United States. This amendment, five years after Lincoln's Emancipation Proclamation, prohibited Slavery or involuntary servitude (except as restitution for a crime) anywhere in the United States of America.

On the heels of the 13th Amendment came the 14th Amendment. The 14th Amendment made those people, who were at one time slaves, citizens of the United States and of the state where in they resided. It further prohibited states

34

from making laws that would abridge the rights
of their citizens.

The 15th Amendment granted citizens the
right to vote. Thus, within a ten year period
the country went from having persons who had no
right to making those persons citizens, prohib-
iting abridgment of their rights and granting
them the right to vote. Unfortunately, the
Civil War had to be fought before that change
took place.

Plessy v. Ferguson

In 1869 an extremely important case was
decided--that of Plessy v. Ferguson. This
case involved separate railroad facilities for
the black population and the white population.
The court, in attempting to justify allowing
separate facilities, suggested there was no
connotation of inferiority or difference in the
facilities. The decision originally concerned
railroad cars and was later extended by
inference to cover everything from bathroom
facilities to education through the concept
that "separate but equal" was acceptable legislation.

Plessy v. Ferguson is actually the first
case specifically articulating the doctrine
that there can be something that is separate
and also equal. And if you can separate railroad
cars which are equal, you can have separate
bathrooms which are equal, and you can have
separate schools which are equal. In fact, as
late as 1928 there was a court case in Mississippi in which the Mississippi School Board said
that a little girl of Chinese heritage was a
person of color and, therefore, was required
to go to the colored school and not to the
white school. This decision was 30 years after
Plessy v. Ferguson and in this case the determination of separate but equal was based generally on color and specifically on the issue of

non-white. All non-white minorities were lumped
together, at least insofar as Mississippi was
concerned, when it came to which school a child
would attend.

These court battles boiled down to the
issue of whether or not states had the right
to regulate activities within their borders and
their confines in circumvention of, for example,
the 14th Amendment to the Constitution. As you
remember, primarily state statutes restricted
the Asian Americans (the Chinese and Japanese)
in California. In the Southwest and Texas,
primarily state statutes were involved in
restrictions of the Hispanics. And to a great
extent state statutes and state laws were used
to restrict the slaves in the South. There has
always been a conflict between the amount of
power that will be vested in the state to maintain its sovereignty and the amount of power
vested in the federal government to maintain
the cohesion and the unity of the nation. It
is a continuing struggle, and it probably will
not end as long as we have the type of government and the type of union that we have. There
will always be the proponents of states' rights
and there will always be proponents of the need
for a strong centralized, federal government.
Hopefully, as time goes by minorities will be
caught less in the middle.

Brown v. The Board of Education of Topeka, Kansas

Brown v. the Board of Education of Topeka,
Kansas was a consolidation of cases in four
states: Kansas, South Carolina, Virginia, and
Delaware. All four states had cases in which
the doctrine of "separate but equal" had been
challenged. In all four the lower courts had
upheld the doctrine and the cases had gone to
the Federal Supreme Court for decision. The
cases were consolidated because the issues were
basically the same; they were decided under the
umbrella of the Brown decision. Brown v. the

36

Board of Education has been called the major
breakthrough in the area of nondiscrimination in
the United States since the 15th Amendment.

The Brown decision said that the doctrine
of "separate but equal," which had been articu-
lated in Plessy v. Ferguson and many subsequent
decisions, no longer had validity, was improper,
incorrect, and would not be utilized in looking
at education in the United States. Part of this
decision had to do with the changes that had
been made in public education over the span of
about 60 years between Plessy and Brown. At
the time of Plessy, public education in the
United States was almost nonexistent; education
in the United States at that time was primarily
private in nature. This is sometimes used as
justification for allowing the concept of
"separate but equal" to be applied to public
education.

The court divided the issues of Brown v.
The Board of Education into two parts. The
court ruled first, in 1954, that "separate but
equal" would not be allowed insofar as public
schools were concerned, and it saved for argument the issue of relief to be granted to the
plaintiffs. Brown II was decided in 1955 with
the opinion written by Chief Justice Earl Warren
speaking to what relief had to be taken to
implement the decision in the first Brown. The
court said it could not supervise or oversee
what happened in the four individual states
concerning the elimination of "separate but
equal" and, therefore, left that task to the
courts in the individual states. The federal
court remanded the individual cases to the states
to deal with the issue of relief with this
language: "The cases are remanded to district
courts to take such preceding and enter such
orders and decrees consistent with this opinion
as are necessary and proper to admit to the
public schools on a racially, nondiscriminatory
basis, with all deliberate speed, the parties in

these cases". (Horowitz and Karst, 1969)

Bowling v. Sharp

The same day as the first Brown decision,
the opinion in the case of Bowling v. Sharp came
down. Bowling v. Sharp applied the decision in
Brown to the District of Columbia. Brown spoke
to the states under the 14th Amendment, which
did not apply to the District of Columbia. In
Bowling v. Sharp the court said that the First
Amendment applied to the District of Columbia
and it offered the same protection vis-a-vis
the District that the 14th Amendment offered to
the states.

The Civil Rights Act of 1964

In the 1960s, the issue of discrimination
on the basis of race, color, or national origin
was dealt with. Two titles in the Civil Rights
Act of 1964 are of particular importance. Title
VI specifically prohibits discrimination on the
basis of race, color, or national origin in any
program receiving federal funds. Title VII
prohibits discrimination in employment on the
basis of race, color, religion, national origin
or sex by any agency or institution with 15 or
more employees. Race, color, religion, and
national origin were included in the original
act; sex was added later.

The Executive Order of 1965

Following the Civil Rights Act of 1964,
came Executive Order 11246 in 1965, signed by
President Lyndon Johnson. This executive order
prohibits discrimination based on race, color,
religion, national origin, or sex in any agency
receiving federal contracts of over $10,000.
It also states that institutions with over 50
employees and federal contracts of over $50,000
must submit a written affirmative action plan
to show how they are going to deal with the

issues of low percentages of women and minorities within the company or institution. (If an organization has less than 50 employees or receives from $10,000 to $50,000 it is required to comply with the executive order but is not required to have a plan on file with the Department of Labor showing how it is going to comply.)

Most current human rights and civil rights protections are follow-up to the act of 1964 and the executive order of 1965.

POST-CIVIL WAR LEGISLATION CONCERNING NATIVE AMERICANS

Between the Civil War and World War II, except for the "gentlemen's agreement" with Japan and the Exclusionary Act with China (discussed in the next section), the federal government was legislating primarily the Native Americans.

Citizenship

The Native Americans were not considered citizens of the United States. They were considered to be conquered people. Because they were not citizens of the United States, they, of course, had none of the protections that were extended with the 13th, 14th, and 15th Amendments to the Blacks in the United States. The Native Americans became citizens primarily through naturalization by treaties which were made with specific tribes. And even with that, the citizenship was very limited. There was not a uniform manner by which Native Americans could become citizens of the United States until 1901. The Native American was in a particularly difficult situation because he or she was not a citizen of any country. The Native American was not like an Irishman who came over and already had Irish citizenship. The Native Americans had no citizenship; citizenship had to be conferred on them specifically by the

federal government. Specific legislation
regarding Indian Citizenship was enacted over
the years following the Civil War. In 1888, a
law was passed that allowed an Indian woman to
become a citizen of the United States if she
married a white man. In 1901, the Dawes Act
was passed and signed. The Dawes Act set up
two criteria for Native Americans to become
citizens: (1) they could become citizens if
they had received an allotment under any other
prior allotment law, either because of removal
or just through the parceling of land within a
given area; or (2) they could become citizens
if they were willing to leave their tribe and
to prove they were living separated and apart
from the tribe, not utilizing any of the protections of the tribal government, and having
established residency in a civilized area. For
Native Americans to become citizens, they had
to divorce themselves from their heritage and
their people. There was one other way Indians
could become citizens: Indian men who fought
in World War I became citizens. Therefore,
Indian women who married white men, Indians
who had received an allotment or who were
willing to separate themselves from their tribe
and live in "civilized society", or Indian men
who fought in World War I were extended
citizenship.

Finally, in 1924, the Citizenship Act was
passed which spoke to all Native Americans and
made all Native Americans citizens.

POST-CIVIL WAR LEGISLATION CONCERNING ASIAN
AMERICANS

The Chinese Americans

In 1863, the California State Board of
Education mandated separate schools for the
Chinese and white children. California, however, didn't build many schools for the minority
children; thus, minority children were largely

uneducated in the state of California for close
to 20 years unless they were educated at home or
in private schools. This situation continued
until 1885 when a judge in San Francisco held
that the 14th Amendment gave the right to a
young Chinese girl to attend public school. She
went to the public school for a period of time
until a Chinese school was built. The new
school was to be for all Orientals--Chinese,
Japanese, and Korean--because at that time the
Japanese and Korean had also begun to enter the
United States.

By 1882 there was a great concern in California about the numbers of Chinese; many people
felt they were flooding the market and becoming
a threat to the laborers in California. Unions
were beginning to grow and organize during this
period, and they felt they could not protect
their workers because they feared the Chinese
would work for lower wages and would accept
poorer working conditions.

The Chinese Exclusionary Acts

On May 6, 1882, the first Chinese Exclusionary Act was passed. This act excluded
Chinese skilled and semi-skilled laborers from
entering this country for a period of ten years.
In 1884, the Act was amended further; the exclusion was extended to merchants and it limited
travel by those Chinese legitimately residing
in the United States prior to 1882 who might
have wanted to return to China to visit. (The
act made it very difficult for these people to
return to the United States after visiting
China even if they could prove they had been
in the United States legally prior to 1882.)
At this time, the burden was on the state to
show that a person was entering the United
States for the first time after 1882 and was,
therefore, one of those to be excluded.

In 1888, the Scott Act further limited

travel by saying that a laborer who visited
China could get back into the United States
only by proving that he had a family here or
that he owned property valued in excess of
$1,000 (which was a great deal of money in 1888).

In 1892, the Gary Act was passed, which
extended the exclusion for another ten years
and placed the burden of proof on the Chinese
that they had been legitimately in the United
States prior to 1882. In 1902, the act was
extended again and it was further amended in
1904 to include the territory of Hawaii: not
only could the Chinese not enter Hawaii, but
those Chinese who were in Hawaii at that time
could no longer enter the United States from
Hawaii. The decisionmakers of California felt
that the Chinese could never be assimilated
into the majority society. They considered the
Chinese an inferior group and felt it was not
beneficial for the state of California to have
those people within its borders.

The Japanese Americans

When the Chinese began to be excluded,
immigration opened for the Japanese. Of all
the ethnic minorities in the United States, the
Japanese were the strongest and most protected.
The reason for this was the strength of their
homeland, Japan, and her policy against immigration. The Japanese government strictly limited
the number of Japanese who were given passports
and allowed to leave the country. Japan was,
therefore, able to furnish her emigrants with
money and passage, and even set up dormitories
and hotels for them in the port cities on the
West Coast. More money appeared to go to the
emigrants going to the West Coast of the United
States than to those stopping in Hawaii.
Japanese immigrants were moving on and basically
working their passage on the basis of indentured
servitude once they reached Hawaii. Unlike the
Chinese, the Japanese entering the United States

42

were for a short period self-sufficient, and
they had money to allow them time to find a good
job.   The Japanese were, therefore, protected
from many of the impositions suffered by other
ethnic minorities in this country.

The Gentlement's Agreement

However, in 1908 it was felt that the
influence of the Japanese was becoming excessive
in California.   Rather than the Exclusionary
Act, as was used against the Chinese, the
Japanese immigration was regulated with the
"gentleman's agreement."   In a memorandum to
President Roosevelt, the Secretary of State
suggested that it probably would not be in the
best interests of the United States to pass an
automatic exclusionary act for the Japanese as
was done for the Chinese.   His reasoning included the following: (1) Japan was ready for war
and had some of the most effective equipment and
personnel existing in the world; (2) The United
States was not ready for war and could not be
ready to meet Japan on equal terms for a long
period.   Thus, the "gentleman's agreement" was
made in 1908 wherein Japan agreed to limit the
number of passports it would grant to skilled
and unskilled Japanese workers, and the United
States agreed not to allow California to have
any restrictive laws relating to the Japanese
already within its borders.

It is interesting to note that at tht turn
of the century, considering the four district
minorities present in the United States--Native
Americans, Blacks, Hispanics, and Asian Ameri-
cans--the group imposed upon the least (the
Japanese) was the one that had the backing of
an extremely strong homeland.   A most important
element in all of this was the strength of the
Japanese government and the unwillingness of
the United States government to antagonize Japan
by passing the arbitrary exclusionary act passed
earlier against the Chinese.   It was possible

43

to work out a mutually acceptable agreement
with the Japanese government to limit the number
of Japanese coming into the Western United
States. That's important because it shows that
our government at that time, and possibly today,
respected and recognized strength. When the
U.S. Government thought it was dealing with
people who were working from a position of
weakness, it generally acted to limit those
people's lives and their participation in the
government. But if there was strength behind
those people, the United States Government was
willing to negotiate.

Executive Order 9066

As a result of the Japanese attack on Pearl
Harbor on December 7, 1941, an act of discrimination occurred that to this day cannot be
justified. Not that other forms of discrimination can be justified, but at least one can say
that slavery existed prior to the inception of
the federal government; that the Native Americans began losing their lands and rights prior
to the existence of federal government; and that
many of the actions taken against the Hispanics
who had settled in the Southwest had been taken
prior to the inception of our federal government.
But what happened after Pearl Harbor was an
action on the part of the United States Government that, in effect, withdrew the protections
of citizenship from a group of American citizens.

The fear of the Japanese on the West Coast
did not start with the rise of Japan in the
1930s. Fear of "the yellow peril" had been
around long before that. The exclusionists
began as early as 1907 to suggest that there
should be fear on the part of the white populus
insofar as the Japanese and Japanese Americans
were concerned. This fear was not a creation
of World War II.

First generation Japanese Americans had

never been allowed to gain American citizenship; they were viewed as citizens of Japan.
Second generation Japanese Americans, however,
were natural-born American citizens. One
would assume they would have no more difficulty
in determining their allegiance when it came to
deciding who their government was for the purpose
of war than second generation Germans or Italians. But for some reason, the federal government decided that both first generation and
second or third generation Japanese Americans
had to be treated in the same manner once the
country was at war with Japan. It was determined that there was no way for the federal
government to decide if a Japanese American was
loyal to the United States, thus they were all
treated as if they were loyal to Japan. On
February 19, 1942, Executive order 9066 was
signed. This order authorized the evacuation
of the West Coast Japanese American population.
They were moved to intermitent areas and then
to relocation centers in most of the western
states.

At the start of World War II, Hawaii was
about 37% Japanese. It is interesting that
Hawaii, which had a high percentage of Japanese
and which you might say logically (if there is
any logic to be found in all of this) had reason
for the most fear since it had been demonstrated
that the islands were capable of being attacked
by the Japanese, used the most counterpressure
to avoid evacuation of their Japanese. It
turned out that only 11 to 12 hundred of the
134,000 Japanese on the islands were ever
removed and brought to the relocation centers
on the mainland.

In spite of all this, there were Japanese
Americans who served the United States with
extraordinary bravery in the armed forces during
World War II. Ironically, the United States,
feared that the Japanese Americans still owed
their allegiance and cultural attachments to

Japan and yet when the U.S. Army attempted to find Japanese American interpreters for use during the war, it was necessary to train great numbers of them to resurrect their facility with their native language. A school was set up in San Francisco, which later had to be moved to Minnesota because of the relocation order, to reschool some Japanese Americans in the Japanese language.

The Japanese were not compensated for the lands they lost when they were relocated, although they were allowed to return after the end of the war. They filed a group damage claim in excess of $300 million dollars and eventually were awarded a little over $1 million. They received about one nickel on the dollar for their damage claim.

SUMMARY

When the federal government felt the threat of a strong Japanese government and the possibility of war over the treatment of Japanese within this country, they overruled the States' attempts to control and limit the Japanese presence in California.

Later during World War I, World War II, and the intermitent state power experienced a resurgence perhaps because the states' needs and desires appeared to coincide with the federal needs and desires. It was not until the Civil Rights Act of 1964 and the Executive Orders of 1965 that the federal government again involved itself in the issues of discrimination on a uniform basis across the country. There were almost a hundred years of wasted time during which the states were working and attempting to control individual minority populations on an individual state basis.

RECENT LEGISLATION CONCERNING ALL MINORITIES

Regents of the University of California v. Bakke

The University of California at Davis Medical School opened in the late 1960s with 50 students and no minorities whatsoever. As the school grew, the numbers of minority students remained nonexistent. Finally a decision was made by the institution to take specific action to insure 16 places for as it was put by the school, "persons of disadvantaged background" (U.S. Commission on Civil Rights, 1979). Thus, sixteen out of 100 students in each new class were primarily minority students.

Bakke, a white male, applied to the medical school two years in a row and was not admitted. He then filed suit saying that the reason he was not admitted was because he had higher credentials than the 16 minorities but lower credentials than the 84 majorities. He further maintained that, under the 14th Amendment, he was being denied equal protection because he was not being considered in the whole block of 100, and that there were minorities who were being given special consideration by virtue of their being minorities.

The important thing to remember is that California had determined that 16 freshmen would be looked at in a different manner. They had decided to take into consideration different issues in determining admission for a certain number of slots although it was also possible that minorities would be admitted who would not have to be considered in this manner.

The Bakke decision is often discussed in the same manner as the Dred Scott decision, in terms of political football. It was a decision like that at the Davis program and made a determination on a set of procedures that were not necessarily reflective of all plans across the country offering opportunities to minorities or disadvantaged persons. Opponents of the Bakke decision also point out that no one really discussed the minorities' interest in the Bakke decision; Davis was busy defending its plan and Bakke was busy defending his rights to go to medical school and no one was addressing the issue of equal opportunity and the issue of recognizing that certain segments of our society had not been given the same opportunity as other segments. The Bakke decision should be considered with those criticisms in mind.

There were six different opinions written between nine justices in the Bakke case. Two opinions were supported by four justices each, and a swing vote was cast by Justice Powell, who wrote his own opinion.

The Stevens Opinion written by Justice Stevens and concurred in by Justices Burger, Stewart and Rehnquist was based solely on the question of whether or not the Davis plan violated Title VI of the 1964 Civil Rights Act. They said that it did because it excluded some persons based on race. They did not address the issue of the 14th Amendment equal protection rights. They said there was no need to get to the question of the 14th Amendment because the case had been decided solely on Title VI.

The Brennen Opinion with White, Marshall, and Backmun concurring said that both Title VI and the 14th Amendment allowed race-conscious steps to be taken to remedy past discrimination. Since the medical school appeared to have discriminated because it had no minorities in its previous classes, the school was merely trying to remedy that situation. In other words, the school could look at the race of certain applicants for admission, recognize that members of certain races had not been given certain opportunities and, therefore, in order to remedy the past discrimination the school could take race-conscious steps to admit minority applicants.

The Bakke decision says in effect that an organization cannot exclude, cannot have quotas, and cannot have percentages for minorities, but it can take into consideration certain race-conscious activities or race-conscious steps in attempting to remedy a situation where minorities have not been represented properly. The school could say, "looking at our population internally as an institution of education, we do not have the numbers of minorities that we should have based on the numbers of minorities in the overall population, and we are going to look at minorities specifically to see if we can remedy the past discrimination."

United Steel Workers of America v. Weber

The decision in United Steel Workers of America v. Weber concerns private enterprise and employee merit rather than education, but the decision is important because it says that organizations can and must make a conscious effort to ensure that the employment of minorities reflects the minority population as a whole in a given area.

Between Weber and Bakke it is almost anyone's guess where the court will go from here in dealing with human and civil rights questions.

TABLE OF CASES

Bolling v. Sharpe, 347 U.S. 497 (1954).

Brown v. Board of Education of Topeka, Kansas, 347 U.S. 483 (1954).

Brown v. Board of Education of Topeka, Kansas, 349 U.S. 274 (1955).

Cherokee Nations v. Georgia, 30 U.S. 256 (1835).

Dred Scott v. Sanford, 60 U.S. 393 (1857).

Johnson and Grahams Leasee v. McIntosh, 21 U.S. 1 (1831).

United Steel Workers of America v. Weber, 61 LED 2nd 480 (1979).

Plessy v. Ferguson, 163 U.S. 393 (1896).

Regents of the University of California v. Bakke, 483 U.S. 265 (1978).

REFERENCES

Horowitz, Harold W. and Karst, Kenneth L. Law, Lawyers and Social Change. New York: Bobbs-Merrill Company, Inc., 1969.

Meier, Matt S. and Rivera, Feliciano. The Chicanos, A History of Mexican Americans. New York: Hill and Wang, 1972.

Melendy, H. Brett. The Oriental Americans. New York: Tayne Publishers, Inc., 1972.

Price, Monroe E. Law and the American Indian. New York: Bobbs-Merrill Company, Inc., 1973.

Rosaldo, Renalto, Calvert, Robert A. and Seligmann, Gustav L. Chicano: The Evolution of a People. Minneapolis: Winston Press, 1973.

U.S. Commission on Civil Rights. <u>Toward an</u>
<u>Understanding of Bakke</u>. Washington D.C.:
U.S. Government Printing Office, 1979.

CHAPTER 3

SCHOOLING AND ITS SOCIAL AND

PSYCHOLOGICAL EFFECTS ON MINORITIES

Lawrence J. Estrada and Melba Vasquez

All too often the multicultural nature of American society has been ignored, and in the past there has been a general failure to recognize the enriching value of diverse cultures and perspectives. Precisely because we are a society of diverse cultures, ethnic groups, and languages, it has been tempting to deny this diversity and to seek, consciously or unconsciously, to promote through educational policy a homogenized citizen, functional to the polity and economy of the dominant society. When faced with manifest cultural and ethnic differences, the national response has perhaps best been characterized by T.S. Eliot's assertion that "humankind cannot bear very much reality."

The coined phrases and presently accepted concepts of bilingualism, biculturalism, multilingual and multicultural education belie years of conflict where minority educators and citizens literally had to fight in order that the American educational system recognize their particular social and cultural worth. This was a fight frequently occluded by educational theory and practices steeped within the philosophy of "cultural deprivation" and class bias. In many parts of the country the fight continues to be waged within school districts and classrooms where minority group students continue to occupy a marginal status within the educational process. Within this chapter the authors will examine a number of the socializing and stratifying effects of schooling upon minority group students in the United States. Attention will be paid to historical, social, and psychological precepts and policy practices that have played critical roles

in the advancement or nonadvancement of minority
children within the American educational system.

Implications for Community Control

Since the inception of the Republic, there
has always been an undeniable concern with
equality in American society. Horace Mann
envisioned the American high school as equally
accessible to all, a place where different social
classes would mix freely, be exposed to the same
curricula and experiences, and have the same
opportunities for success in the growing economy.
Later reformers gave up this idea partly because
all children were not getting into or finishing
high school; they considered it more important
to get all children into school and keep them
there longer than to have the children take the
same courses. Of course, the differentiation of
schooling tended to serve changing industrial
needs and was a necessity for stricter social
control throughout the period of heavy immigration, labor organization, and left-wing agitation
in the labor movement during the beginning of the
19th century. To satisfy the concern for social
unity while preserving the class structure,
differentiation was organized within the same
school. As Spring (1972) points out, the concept
of equality as intrepreted by the reformers
included the ideal democracy that brought people
from different classes together in the same
institution: "the comprehensive high school was
to give them common ideas, common ideals, and
common modes of thought, feeling, and action
that made for cooperation, social cohesion, and
social solidarity." Since students were separated into different courses, other means of
creating a sense of unity and equality among the
groups was necessary; thus different social
classes of students were mixed through extra-
curricular activities, such as athletics, social
clubs, and school government.

Within this context equality was only a

54

facade; it had little to do with the reality of the school or the reality of the economic and social structure. Once out of school, the sharing of common experiences by members of different social groups ceased. Furthermore, with a large internal migration of Blacks and Mexican Americans to northern and western urban areas after World War II, racial and ethnic conflicts became too great to overcome with a false sense of unity in the school systems.

The school system, as reformed in the early 20th century with its notions of free and universal education to all citizens, ran into serious problems by the 1960s. Twenty years of rapid post-war economic growth had produced little change in income distribution. Education was still distributed along class lines, a situation that became increasingly unacceptable to Blacks, Chicanos, Puerto Ricans, and Native Americans, to whom the progressive definition of "equal opportunity" left them at the bottom of the educational and vocational ladder. To them, centralized control by Anglo school boards was a major factor to blame, and in some communities a struggle began for community control of schools, teacher selection, and curriculum related to cultural content.

In addition to the growing unrest with American schooling posed by minority groups in the 1960s, many upper middle-class whites were not satisfied with the schools either: they rejected the corporate structure and the transmission of that structure and its values through the school. Those parents pushed for child center schools which stressed interpersonal relations rather than extrinsic rewards. This concept is best expressed by Carnoy (1974) in his treatise Education as Cultural Imperialism: "in a more general framework we see two significant challenges to the existing social order. First, there are demands that the school satisfy their rhetorical goals of providing equal education

55

opportunities (read as equal educational outcomes) for all groups in society, rich and poor, black and white, Chicano and Anglo. This objective has implications for the financing, heterogenety of enrollments, and educational offerings of the schools. Second, the schools are being pressured to be client oriented rather than professionally oriented, child centered rather than adult centered. This goal has implications for the number and nature of alternatives that must be available to satisfy the needs of students with substantially different talents, personalities, abilities, and interests."

During the late sixties and seventies most Blacks, Chicanos, and Puerto Ricans as well as Native Americans began demanding that the schools make them more employable in the present economic structure; that the schools increase their status within the dominant society; and that the schools recognize their community control movement fits into the challenge of equal school outcomes. Minority groups believe correctly that white, Anglo control has created schools in which their children cannot do as well as those of the controlling interests; therefore, control is essential to equal opportunity and learning within the school system. Control, however, is an elusive entity. Where Blacks and Chicanos have gained control of the boards of ghetto and barrio schools, for example, they have found that they do not control the state legislature, which distributes state aid to education and sets curriculum and other requirements. But even if minorities could get equal funds out of the legislature, even if they could later curriculum as they have tried in numerous instances, even if they could produce equal outcomes through community control, they still would not control the economy in requirements for jobs. They would remain dependent for the definition of social roles on a society that has continually insured them the bottom rung on its ladder.

Winning at least some control over one's destiny, however, especially for a people who have been oppressed during their entire history in this country, does have valuable psychological effects. Political and social learning as a result of community control may not be the end of a liberation period but the beginning of something much more extensive and profound, depending on who controls the community control movement. Cooptation by establishment Blacks and Chicanos would ensure that the building of self identity and the use of the schools for real community social change and political development be subverted to the needs of the controlling structure. In such a case, oppressed minorities would successfully maintain their undesireable social roles through their "own school boards". The results of community control of schools in essence are intrinsically tied to the dependency of the community on decisions presently out of its grasp. To fully comprehend the ongoing conflict between minority groups, community control and the American school system, it is imperative to reexamine the historical, socio/ psycho context from which educational policy was produced and implemented. From this perspective one may be able to understand the tenuous and subordinate position that most minority school children still hold within the American classroom.

Minorities and Educational Stratification

Zimbardo (1979) defines "prejudice" as the learned beliefs, attitudes, and values held by one person about others that: 1) are formed on the basis of incomplete information, 2) are relatively immune to contrary informational input, 3) make a categorical assignment of individuals to certain classes or groups that are typically negatively valued. Prejudice is thus the internal state or psychological set to react in a biased way toward members of certain groups.

Discrimination is the behavior that prejudice gives rise to. While prejudice is carried
by individuals, "racism" is perpetuated across
generations by laws and treaties, group norms
and customs. It is carried by newspapers,
textbooks, and other media.

The effects of racism and prejudice have
taken their toll upon the egalitarian principles
of American education advocated in the early
part of the century. Americanization, a term
long associated with the elusive search for
national homogeneity and unity, became almost
synonymous with intolerance of cultural and
ethnic differences falling out of the mainstream
of white, Anglo society. This intolerance
carried over to the classroom and more often
than not formed the basis for educational
policies that were both adverse to minorities
and paramount in the inadequate attention and
empathy afforded by educators to educational
issues and problems affecting minority groups.
(Cremin, 1976) The educational history of most
non-white minority groups in this country during
the 20th century has been, unfortunately, one
of neglect and misunderstanding. In spite of
legal precedents and breakthroughs in more
recent times "insuring fair and equal education",
minorities during the decades of the fifties,
sixties and well into the seventies received
unequal and discriminatory education.

Segregation, long associated with education
in the South and its nefarious effects upon the
educational and intellectual development of the
Black school child, took on new significance in
Northern urban centers and in the Southwest.
Urban ghetto schools as well as rural schools in
small Southwestern cities shared a common bond
of inadequate resources, ill prepared teachers
and often times stringent educational policies
and practices that relegated them to their own
"type" of education. In many parts of the
Southwest it was common practice for schools to

place children with distinguishable Spanish
surnames in classrooms separate from children
with non-Spanish names. These were often called
"Mexican" rooms. The schools justified this
action by claiming that if one placed children
who did not speak English together in the same
classroom, they would somehow learn the new
language more quickly than if they were placed
in a room with English-speaking children. Often
the educators overlooked the fact that many
children with Spanish surnames did not speak
Spanish at all. (Carter and Segura, 1979)

By and large, segregated education for all
minority school children was inferior to the
instruction given to other children. This form
of separatism created attitudes of inferiority
within the minority child and of superiority
within the minds of Anglo children. Possibly of
greater consequence was the fact that it reinforced the stereotypes and corollaries of educators who felt that minority children were in need
of different and more basic forms of education
suited to their "temperament and abilities."
(Weinberg, 1977)

In conjunction with segregated education,
many school districts in the Southwest and even
those schools situated on Indian reservations
were to enact "English only" laws which would
prohibit the usage of Spanish or any Native
American languages within the confines of the
school premises. A number of states up until
the early sixties prohibited the use of any form
of non-English instruction. Furthermore, many
children who could not speak English were punish-
ed, sometimes physically, for speaking their own
language in the classroom or on the school
grounds. This reprehensible practice in some
parts of the Southwest continues to persist.
Cities such as El Paso, Texas; Tucson, Arizona;
and Santa Anna, California actually had school
bylaws that spelled out the practice of dismissal
for both students and teachers who utilized

Spanish within the classroom or on school grounds. (Estrada and Nava, 1976)

The failure of the school system to meet the needs of minority school children can be illustrated in a number of other ways. In large school districts in cities such as Chicago, Boston, San Antonio and Los Angeles, gerrymandering took place in order to separate Blacks and Chicanos from the dominant society through changes in the political boundaries defining the school district. This manipulation of school district boundaries assured the poor, and in particular Blacks and Chicanos, that their schools would be inferior to those of the more affluent population. The difference in quality was simply a matter of the difference in the funds available for the operation of the respective schools. The funds to run a school in the fifties and sixties depended solely on the value of the property in which the school district was located and the property taxes collected. Thus, the "Anglo" schools generally had more money for materials, equipment, school buildings, and teacher's salaries than schools located in poorer neighborhoods. Although efforts have been made by many cities to redefine school boundaries so as to insure greater equity within urban educational settings and to change the entire tax base for school funding, many school districts across the nation still maintain racially and ethnically divided school districts reinforced by political boundaries. (Weinberg, 1977)

The melting pot corollary of American society, long a standard and major objective of American education, has come under fire by a number of educators. (Bowles and Gintis, 1977; Carnoy, 1974; Spring, 1976) They have vociferously assailed the duality of American education, which on the other hand purports double standard of education for majority and minority group students. These educators view American education as an inculcating device for majority group values

and norms and as a means for maintaining a status
quo that relegates all minorities to an inferior
status within society along with lessened expectations and a rejection of their cultural worth.
An examination of theoretical notions, proposi-
tions and possible alternatives within education
may aid in clarifying this rather apparent duality.

The Effects of Personality and
Culture on School Achievement

What are the effects of ethnic minority
cultures on the educational attainment of ethnic
persons in this country? Many discussions imply
that identification with values, attitudes and
behaviors of the Chicano culture for example, is
a liability to educational achievement and that
aculturation--the process of "giving up" of
one's subculture and adapting to the values,
attitudes and behaviors of the majority culture--
should be the guiding philosophy of educational
programming and interventions. (Schwartz, 1969;
Madsen, 1964; Heller, 1968) This section is not
intended to review studies identifying cultural
traits affecting educational attainment, but
rather to describe three models which have been
described to view the interaction of culture and
schooling.

The Cultural Deficit Model

Much of the more recent literature describing the interaction of culture and education has
been necessarily a reaction to the cultural
deficit model. This model holds that the cultures of some ethnic groups (particularly
Chicanos, Native Americans, and Blacks) interfere
with the education attainment and intellectual
and emotional development of children. There are
various problems with the writings of such work.
Guthrie (1976) critiqued two studies including
the Moynihan Report, The Negro Family: The Case
for National Action (1965), by pointing out that

61

the reports concentrated almost solely on what was termed "negative" in the Black experience. Both studies declared that the principle sources of scholastic failure of Black children stemmed not from the schools but rather from the student's home environment and family background. Guthrie (1976) critiques the assumptions from the reports as "gross over-simplifications of the data compiled" and points out the authors' failure to comprehend the practical adaptation to a racist environment confronting the average Black family. Guthrie further questions the methodology and experimenter bias of the reports.

Hernández (1970) and Vaca (1970) similarly review and critique the works of several social scientists that present distorted, negative views of the Mexican American culture. Hernandez points out that researcher bias, inadequacy and inappropriateness of theoretical framework, sophistry and irrationality, inappropriateness and subjectivity of survey techniques, and misinterpretation of findings can have a destructive effect by further alienating ethnic groups and perpetuating false, derogatory stereotypic characteristics.

Romano (1969) points out that Kluckhohn and Strobeck (1961), for example, base a description of Hispanics in New Mexico on a sample of 23 in a community of 150 persons and generalize about New Mexican value orientations. According to Hernandez's review, Heller's subsequent study of Mexican Americans relies heavily on the Kluckhohn sample of 23. Both studies, as well as others, treat Mexican Americans as ahistoric and as needing to be aculturated in order to be considered equal members of American society.

<u>The Cultural Difference Model</u>

It is only in the past decade that such poorly conducted research has been challenged. Unfortunately, the stereotypic portrayals of ethnic groups have been taken for truth, built on and perpetuated by social scientists for several decades. New research that identifies cultural differences must reexplain traits or characteristics that have previously been described as deficient. However, the assumption of the cultural difference model, that culturally different populations can be compared on the same instrument, has been challenged.

One of the most hotly debated issues in the attempt to explain the poor educational performance of ethnic minority students revolves around I.Q. tests. The discussion of the effects of schooling on minorities cannot be complete without this issue.

Sanchez (1934) was one of the first to point out the misapplication of psychological and academic tests, particularly with bilingual children. He challenged the lack of validity of I.Q. tests by pointing out that a test is valid only if the items of the test are as common to each child tested as they were to the children upon whom the norms were based. Yet the tests continued to be misused by the placement of Chicano/Latino students in special education classes when their intelligence was actually average or even superior.

Five decades after Sanchez's indictment, very little progress has been made in the more appropriate use of standardized testing with minority students. Sedlacek and Brooks (1976) have been critical of the methodology used by studies which purport that use of standardized tests with Blacks and other minorities is valid. They particularly question the use of standardized tests to predict which students are likely to succeed academically.

Mercer (1977) addresses the Americanization process referred to earlier which provide insight to current test practices. Mercer (1977) states

"... the implicit goal of public education was to produce monolingual, monocultural, Anglicized children and to allow non-anglo cultural traditions to die." Mercer concludes that since all standardized tests are designed to predict those children likely to succeed in school, the values of anglicization are implicit in standardized tests geared to the public schools. This misuse of tests has thus restricted the educational opportunities of minority students by placing disproportionate members in tracts which restrict their true potential.

Research that looks at cultural differences can be helpful if conducted appropriately. For example, in an extensive review of work examining motivational constructs of Mexican American children, Kagan (1977) concludes that Mexican American children are more concerned than other children with cooperative motives, especially group enhancement and altruism. When presented with behavior alternatives across a number of situations, Chicano children chose alternatives which seem to satisfy cooperative motives rather than competitive motives more often than other children. The findings of such studies as those Kagan reviewed have practical implications for public institutions. For example, rather than discriminate against Mexican American children who may be less competitive and more group oriented, educators could plan educational programs around the traits characterizing the learner.

Studies that do focus on cultural differences must be conducted appropriately and interpretations of such work must take into account, for example, the problems associated with using the same standardized tests with all groups. Finally, care must be taken to prevent further promotion of stereotypes and generalizations.

LaBelle (1976) goes further in describing a contextual approach to understanding behavior.

In the case of education, for example, rather than simply gathering data about the ethnic minority student and comparing it to Anglo behavior using the same standardized tests, LaBelle believes that educators must give priority attention to the practices of the school in interaction with the students.

Mercer's (1977) System of Multi-cultural Pluralistic Assessment (SOMPA) offers a pluralistic assessment based on the assumption that ethnic groups have not conformed to the Anglo model, and that here is a complex system of cultural and structural pluralism today. While it would be difficult to discuss Mercer's approach in detail here, it should suffice to say that such pluralistic assessment approaches will hopefully open up opportunities for minority students.

In regard to research, Martínez (1978) states:

> Human behavior can be understood only if it is viewed within the cultural context in which it occurs. We might call this approach cultural relativisim. Psychological formulations that adequately explain the behaviors of Anglos within the Anglo culture may not necessarily explain the behaviors of Chicanos within the Chicano culture. Thus, a situation exists where improperly applied explanations of the behavior of Chicanos may actually do them harm.

School settings may, therefore, benefit the learning of Chicano and other ethnic minority students by accomodation curriculum practices to best meet the learning needs of these students.

In summary, social scientists have previously utilized the cultural deficit model to interpret findings (often applying inappropriate methodology) in an ethnocentric and damaging manner. Both the "cultural difference" and "contextual" models can contribute to increasing understanding and modification of curriculum practices to help ethnic minority students. Educators and researchers might, however, rather than simply identify cultural traits to categorize groups, begin to assess and promote effective learning experiences for ethnic minority students.

Psychological Effects of Prejudice and Racism

Social psychologists who examine the effects of prejudice, discrimination, and racism on individuals within groups point out that an individual's self-esteem or sense of worth is primarily the result of individual feedback about one's personal worth and competence, but also results from cultural feedback of the legitimacy of the person's primary reference group. (Zimbardo, 1979)

Individuals who are members of an ethnic minority group in this country thus experience rejection often through subtle patterns of prejudice that ignore one's existence as well as through more hostile, obvious acts of discrimination.

Unfortunately, if an individual accepts--consciously or subconsciously--the negative stereotypes of one's primary identity group, a tendency may be to try and disassociate from one's "despised" group. Some behavioral examples of such disassociation include name changes, hair straightening, rejection of language, family, friends and peers. This insidious process often causes a person to turn against one's self as well, and results in psychological damage to one's self-esteem and identity.

66

The sources of negative feedback and messages
about this country's ethnic minority groups are
pervasive and insidious. The U.S. Commission of
Civil Rights (1973) illustrated, for example, the
existence of negative teacher attitudes and expectations toward Mexican American children. Using
a modified version (to specify ethnicity) of
Flanders Interaction Analysis Categories, the
Commission attempted to determine how patterns
of classroom behaviors vary with different types
of teachers and students, specifically possible
disparities in the way teachers treat Mexican
American and Anglo students within the same
classroom. Classroom observation was conducted
in schools in California, New Mexico, and Texas.
Within each state, geographical areas were selected that included rural, urban, and suburban
schools in which large numbers of Mexican American
students were enrolled. Fifty-two schools were
randomly sampled; 494 English classes at fourth,
eighth, tenth, and twelfth grades were observed.

Disparities of teacher interaction with
Mexican American and Anglo students were found in
six of the twelve categories identified. The
categories where significant differences were
found included: praising or encouraging, acceptance or use of student ideas, questioning, positive student response, all noncriticizing teacher
talk, and all student speaking. The Commission
reports:

> Mexican-American pupils in the
> survey areas receive considerably
> less of some of the most education-
> ally beneficial forms of teacher
> behavior than do Anglos in the same
> classrooms. Mexican-Americans receive
> significantly less praise and encour-
> agement from the teacher and less
> often hear the teacher accept or
> use the ideas they express. Teachers
> also spend significantly less time
> in asking questions of Chicano pupils

than of Anglo pupils. On a com-
posite measure of positive response
from the teacher, which includes
acceptance of student feelings,
praise or encouragement, and
acceptance of student ideas,
Mexican-Americans receive signif-
icantly less than Anglos. . . The
six statistically significant
disparities in classroom interaction all favor Anglo pupils over
Chicano pupils.

In describing the effect of this differen-
tial teacher/student interaction upon a Mexican
American student, the Commission points to the
influence of teacher expectations of students
and their reactions to student behavior. The
results indicate that teachers are likely to
have negative attitudes and expectations towards
Mexican Americans and to treat these students
inappropriately in the classroom.

Educators interested in modifying the
effects of such expectations can aid in the
inoculation of young people who are targets of
such prejudice by establishing a sense of pride
in their origins, history and group identity.
While no single approach to the educational
problems of the culturally different can achieve
significant results, multiethnic and multicultural programs can foster a creative multicultural
self-image to displace those negative images that
students acquire, Estrada and Nava (1967) point
out that:

. . . the child must be secure
and . . . the value orientations
the school imparts should fulfill
the expectations he has already
learned. To the Chicano this means
his cultural heritage and linguistic
background must be understood by the
school and academically reinforced

by the school.

SUMMARY

The attempts to provide equitable schooling
for ethnic minorities have been in actuality a
facade, having little to do with the realities
of the differences in economic and social structure. The consequential unrest and discontent
has resulted in the establishment of community
control. The effectiveness of the attempts to
win control over one's destiny is psychologically
valuable.

Educational goals and policy were produced
from a specific historical, sociological, and
psychological context. The development of the
Americanization process in the schools, for
example, has resulted in the disenfranchisement
and oppression of non-Anglo groups who have
retained their cultural values, languages and
attitudes. American education has, in fact, been
highly criticized for its dual standard--purport-
ing equality for all students while relegating
inferior status to minorities for failing to
adopt majority group values and norms.

In addition, three models were described to
view the various descriptions by social scientists
of interaction of culture and schooling: (1) the
cultural deficit model; (2) the cultural difference model; and (3) the contextual model. The
cultural deficit model has categorized those
findings that interpret data in an ethnocentric
and destructive manner. The cultural difference
approach can be helpful in identifying different
cognitive styles, values and language in developing appropriate curriculum practices, but is also
critiqued on the basis of its assumptions that
different populations can be measured on the same
instrument. The contextual model prioritizes
observing behavior in the context of a situation
and thus assessing the effects of such interaction. Mercer's SOMPA is an example of a

pluralistic assessment which provides the opportunity to take cultural differences into account
for ability testing.

Finally, the effects of prejudice, discrimination and racism on individuals were described.

The psychological damage resulting from the
covert or overt negative messages about the
legitimacy of one's primary identity group is
pervasive and insidious. Only through pride in
origins, history and group identity, can the
negative effects be modified.

Use of pluralistic assessment will help in
the more appropriate identification of the true
potential of ethnic minority students. Curricula
which take into account the cognitive and learning styles, language and values of diverse
cultures in addition to the Anglican is a much
more realistic and healthy approach for ethnic
minority students. Teaching and promoting the
history, values, languages and heritage of
diverse cultures will not only help innoculate
ethnic minority students against the negative
messages in society, but also enrich learning for
nonminority students. If public education is to
continue to purport equality of education for
all, a multicultural approach to the socializa-
tion process must be incorporated.

REFERENCES

Bowles, S. and Gintis, H. Schooling in Capitalist America. New York: Basis Book, Inc., 1976

Carnoy, M. Education as Cultural Imperialism. New York: David McKay Co., 1974.

Carnoy, M. Schooling in a Corporate Society. New York: David McKay Co., 1972.

Carter, T. P. and Segura, R. D. Mexican-Americans in School: A Decade of Change. New York: College Entrance Examination Board, 1979.

Estrada, L. J. and Nava, A. "The Long Struggle for Bilingualism and a Consistent Language Policy: Early Childhood Education in California and the Southwest", UCLA Educator, 1976, 19 (1), 36-41.

Guthrie, R. V. Even the Rat was White: A Historical View of Psychology. New York: Harper & Row, 1976.

Heller, C. S. Mexican-American Youth: Forgotten Youth at the Crossroads. New York: Random House, 1968.

Hernández, D. Mexican American Challenge to a Sacred Cow: A Critical Review and Analysis Focusing on Two UCLA Graduate School of Education Research Studies about Mexican American "Values" and Achievement. Monograph #1, Los Angeles: University of California, Chicano Studies Center, 1970.

Kagan, S. Social Motives and Behaviors of Mexican-American and Anglo-American Children. In J. L. Martínez, Jr. (ed.) Chicano Psychology. New York: Academic Press, 1977, pp. 45-86.

Kluckhohn, F. R. and Strodbeck, F. L. Variations in Value Orientations. New York: Row, Peterson & Co., 1961.

LaBelle, J. T. Defecit, Difference and Contestual
Explanations for the School Achievement of
Students from Minority Ethnic Backgrounds. UCLA
Educator, 1976, 19 (1), 25-29.

Madsen, W. Mexican-Americans of South Texas:
Case Studies in Cultural Anthropology. New York:
Holt, Rinehart and Winston, 1964.

Martínez, J. L., Jr. (ed.). Chicano Psychology.
New York: Academic Press, 1977, pp. 11-16.

Mercer, J. R. Identifying the Gifted Chicano
Child. In J. L. Martínez, Jr. (ed.). Chicano
Psychology. New York: Academic Press, 1977,
pp. 155-174.

Romano-V, O, I. The Anthropology and Sociology
of the Mexican-Americans: The Distortion of
Mexican-American History. El Grito. 2 (1),
1968, pp. 13-26.

Sanchez, G. I. Bilingualism and Mental Measures:
A Word of Caution, Journal of Applied Psychology,
1934, 18, 765-772.

Schwartz, A. J. A comparative Study of Values and
Achievement: Mexican-American and Anglo Youth.
Sociology of Education, 1971, 44, 438-462.

Sedlacek, E. and Brooks, G. C., Jr. Racism in
American Education: A Model for Change.
Chicago: Nelson Hall, Inc., 1976.

Spring, J. The Sorting Machine. New York: David
McKay Co., 1976.

Spring, J. "Education and the Corporate State",
Socialist Revolution, No. 8 March-April, 1972.

U.S. Commission on Civil Rights. Mexican-American
Education Study, Report II. The Unfinished
Education: Outcomes for Minorities in the Five
Southwestern States. Washington, D.C.: U.S.

Government Printing Office, 1971.

Vaca, N. C. The Mexican-American in the Social Sciences. El Grito, 1970, 4 (1), pp. 17-51.

Weinberg, M. A Chance to Learn. New York: Cambridge University Press, 1977.

Weinberg, M. Minority Students: A Research Appraisal. Washington, D.C.: H. E. W., 1977.

Zimbardo, P. G. The Social Bases of Behavior. Psychology and Life (10th ed.) Glenview, Ill.: Scott, Foresman and Co., 1979, 624-655.

PART II

APPROACHES TO MULTICULTURAL EDUCATION

CHAPTER 4

FOLKLORE: SOME EDUCATION EFFECTS

William E. Sims

The use of folklore and literature of
minorities can be considered an innovative
approach to the increase in awareness and understanding of school personnel. Minorities use
folklore to speak of many things in many ways.
As middle class teachers and their students
listen to the voices of minorites, speaking
through folklore they will gain a better background and history of today's racial situation.
Folklorists are analytical and offer new perspectives on culturally different problems.

The folklorists investigate the life and
spirit of cultural groups by studying their
customs, stories, jokes and myths. They are
concerned with humanity, with life, as revealed
by the great story tellers in varous cultural
groups.

AMERICAN FOLKLORE

Under the heading of American folklore can
be found many different types of ethnic folklore.
For this paper we will discuss white American
folklore, Black American folklore, Hispanic
folklore, Native American folklore, and Asian
American folklore, which have several divisions.
White American folklore, is the best known. It
has many aspects; there are heroes and heroines
that have served to inspire young white students
to great deeds. Like all folklore many of the
stories started as "real life" exploits of brave
and heroic men and women. However, the stories
were embellished over a period of time and the
heroes and heroines became folk legends.

It is safe to say that middle class white
Americans have made excellent use of folklore in

the educational system, folk heroes and heroines
have become major models for young people. Middle
class Americans have used folklore to grant status
to generations of Americans. Take for example
the office of president of the United States; this
is a status position, and thousands of young boys
grow up wanting to enjoy the prestige of being
president of America. The myths, folktales and
true stories surrounding some of America's presidents, such as: the myth that George Washington
never told a lie; the stories about Teddy Roosevelt as the leader of, and a great rough rider;
John F. Kennedy's profiles of courage; all of
these stories have in a sense become a part of
American folklore, and they inspire white youth.
Stories are told, about the great presidents, to
young boys that are part fact, part fiction, and
they permit the young boys to dream that they can
occupy America's most lofty position in the not-
to-distant future if they are honest, brave, and
determined.

These dreams of aspirations are closed to
young women and minorities, because America never
had a woman, Black, Hispanic, Asian American, or
Native American president. American folklore concerned with the office of president has served its
best educational purpose for young white boys.
Each boy, if he is white, believes that it does
not matter what the circumstance of his birth; nor
does it matter how humble his beginnings, he can
aspire to the presidency. He has heard the folk-
tale about Abraham Lincoln's log cabin birthplace,
and about Andrew Jackson's humble beginnings.
These folktales in a sense are as detrimental to
minority youth as they are inspiring to white
youth, because they say clearly to the minority,
"you can never reach this status in the American
social system": this position is reserved for
American white only, and that has been true.
History has supported this unwritten policy, and
since all children must study American history
they find the folktales that they have heard reinforced by over two hundred years of history.

For contrast a look at another historical figure from white American folklore is worth perusal. Children grow up in America listening to stories about baseball, the all American sport, and about great baseball players. For more than a hundred and fifty years white boys patterned themselves after legendary white baseball players. The greatest of all, and one surrounded by myths was, of course, the immortal Babe Ruth. On playgrounds all over the land, one could hear boyish voices saying "I'm Babe Ruth." Since Babe Ruth was white, flamboyant and famous, he served as an inspiration for white youth.

BLACK AMERICAN FOLKLORE

There were no Black major league players, no Mexican players, no Asian players, no Native American players for most of baseball's history, who were recognizable. The folklore worked to the advantage of white youth and to the disadvantage of minorities. For years minority youth played baseball because it was America's pastime, not because they believed they could ever play professionally in the major leagues. All of the stories that they were told were about legendary figures who were white.

In the 1930's a few baseball stars emerged from the Black American society, these heroes and their folk stories replaced, for Black youth, the stories of white players. With this impetus Black youth became more involved, they took as their inspiration, the Black players that were talked about in glorious terms, the Josh Gibson's and Sachel Paige's. These success stories inspired and made believers of Jackie Robinson and Willie Mays, Hank Brown and Larry Doby. Look at baseball today, the American pastime is comprised of a multiethnic/multicultural assortment of players. The management of baseball has also changed with minorities now serving as managers in an athletic endeavor that less than forty years ago was closed to them.

A not too easily understood phenomenon of
Black people in America is the role played by
women in the Black community. In these days when
women in general are striving to become liberated,
Black women are not overly concerned; they have
never been subjugated by Black men, only by a
white society. Folklore has played an important
part in the feeling of independence and freedom
that Black women in America have. Down through
the years Black girls have heard the folktales of
the majestic African queens, who were reveried
not because they were linked to African Kings,
but because they were rulers in their own right.
Stories about slavewomen in America are very
descriptive in their use of the term "regal"
when referring to female slaves. Often the word
"proud" is also used when the Black slave woman is
discussed. Little Black girls were persuaded by
their mother to walk with pride; they were told
"you descended from African queens."

The folk heroine Sojourner Truth served as
an inspiration to generations of Black girls,
who patterned themselves after the leading female
Black abolitionist. They committed to memory the
stories of how Sojourner used her great intellect
and caustic wit to turn an often hostile crowd
into a supportive coalition for the freedom of
Black people. The Sojourner Truth stories made
it clear to young girls that intelligence, guile,
forcefulness and determination were virtues that
would prove beneficial to Black women in America.

Another Black heroine, Harriett Tubman, contributed to the moral fiber of Black women in
America. Many stories were told of her exploits.
Little girls were enthalled with stories of her
daring, bravery, stamina, and toughness. Black
girls would hang on every word about the most
celebrated Black "conductor" on the famous under-
ground railroad. Black people are great story-
tellers, they come from an oral history tradition,
and they would dramatically describe the "close
calls" that Harriett had on her nineteen trips to

78

the South to lead more than three hundred slaves
to freedom. Whispering, and speaking slowly for
the proper emphasis, at the important part of the
story they would emphasize that Harriett Tubman
had a price on her head of forty thousand doll-
ars, but she was skillful and was never captured,
nor did she ever lose a "passenger" entrusted
to her.

It is not an accident of circumstance that
the great leaders of the Civil Rights movement
were Black ministers. American Black folklore
is replete with stories about the Black preacher.
Folklore and Black religion are interwoven and
became an important force in the lives of slaves;
many of them found strength and meaning in their
churches. The Black preacher was the spokesman
for his people in 1787, when the first all-Negro
church was founded, and he is the spokesman for
his people in 1980. (Fishel and Quarles 1967)

The Black church produced Richard Allen, the
first national Black leader, and president of
the first Black convention held in American
history. The convention was held in Philadelphia
in 1830 "to devise ways and means for bettering
the Black condition." (Hamilton 1972) The Black
church also produced Denmark Vesey, the developer
of a formidable conspiracy to free his people.
Vesey was a brilliant mulatto; he read widely
and spoke freely, rebuking fellow Blacks who
demonstrated servility. In the Black church he
reminded his fellows of how the Israelites dealt
with the captured city of Jericho, after the walls
came tumbling down: "And they utterly destroyed
all that was in the city, both man and woman,
young and old, and ox, and ass, with the edge of
the sword and they burned the city." (Rose 1976)

The Black church also produced Nat Turner,
restless, inquisitive, and observant, Nat learned
to read quickly and was admitted to religious
services in his master's household. From his
prayers, fasts and revelations from the Lord, Nat

79

was convinced, he declared, "that I was ordained for some great purpose in the hands of the Almighty." A short, coal-black man, Turner was fearless, honest, temperate, and extremely intelligent. (Blassingame 1979)

The Black preachers that we have briefly described are an integral part of American Black folklore, and they served as role models for a later generation of Black preachers who in their way are serving Black people as leaders. The early Black preachers were masters of the vivid phrase, folk poetry, and picturesque words. Described by many white observers as "rude eloquence" and "genuine oratory", the sermons of Black preachers excited the emotions. They were orations in which "exposition was not attempted." Description, exhortation, appeal formed the warp and woof. (Blassingame 1979)

The folktales passed down from father to son glorifying the Black preacher served to motivate young Black boys to select a life of service to their ethnic group. Unlike the unlettered ministers of the early Black church, succeeding generations of Black preachers were students of theology, they completed degree programs at some of America's best colleges and universities. Not only were Black boys influenced by the stories that were told to them about Black preachers, they could see these men in their communities. The minister was a very visible person. In the early days of American Black history the preacher was the man of their ethnic group who could read, he was neat, wore a shirt and tie, generally had the respect of both white and Black people. He was present in the home when there was trouble and sorrow, he was there in time of gayety. Many of the early Black preachers had another more direct appeal to Black youth. Their militancy appealed to the masses. These volatile ministers used their pulpits to speak of freedom and retribution against an oppressive system. They were resourceful, and used their sermons to address the wretchedness of slavery. The Black preacher presented his sermon successfully, because he was a master of rhythm and power. He worked with a storehouse of phrases and ideas. He was able to establish an emotional rapport between himself and his congregation.

Black people then and now are very close to their ministers. You seldom hear the masses of Black people speak of "my lawyer" or "my doctor" or even "my country". These terms are not foreign to them; the masses do use professional services, but when they use "my" in connection with a person, place, or thing it has a special meaning to them. They say lovingly "my home", "my car", "my brother", "my pastor". The phrase "my pastor" has a strong sense of mutual, personal attachment. (Hamilton 1979)

The nuances of Black American folklore and religion were not wasted on Black youth; they were absorbed. If folklore had not acquainted young Black people with the lives of Richard Allen, Henry Highland Garnet, Denmark Vesey, and Nat Turner, Black America would never have produced Martin Luther King, Ralph Abernathy, Andrew Young, Malcolm X, and Jesse Jackson.

HISPANIC FOLKLORE

Hispanic folklore in America has two parts: the Spanish and the Mexican-Indian. Originally one heritage, unified in time, they are now separated. The Spanish-speaking have often complained that little is known about them, which is true, and that their problems have received little attention by the larger American public. A distinguished spokesman for the Spanish-speaking, once referred to them as "an orphan group, the least sponsored, and the least vocal large minority group in the nation". (McWilliams 1974) Hispanic folklore has had a lot to do with the docility of Hispanics.

81

Hispanics in America are no longer docile and non-competitive, but they arrived late on the human rights protest scene. For generations they have heard the stories of how a few companies of Spanish soldiers, crudely armed, conquered Mexico. The Spanish transplanted their language, which they used to glorify Spanish heroes: Columbus, Magellan, Balboa, Cortez, and Coronado. They also brought with them their religion, which they used to instill in the natives: "love your enemies, and turn the other cheek." Religion and folklore cannot be separated, and it is significant that the Spaniards built missions throughout the country. It was in these missions that stories, religious stories, were told to enhance the peace loving philosophy of the natives.

The close interlocking relationship between the church and the family has helped to perpetuate docility and respect for authority among Hispanic people. Authority rests with the priest, the patron and the male head of the family. Institutionalized leadership, and not personal leadership tended to be non-competitive. Folktales in Mexico supported this philosophy of cooperation and compliance and it will take many years for Hispanic people to rid themselves of this cultrual inbreeding. This is not as easy as it sounds, because Hispanics are caught between a rock and a hard place. They love the stories about the Spanish dons and their explorations, but they are also aware that the Spanish dominated the larger Mexican-Indian culture.

Hispanic folklore has more than a sprinkling of fantasy woven into the fabric. The often repeated tales of how Spanish grandes and caballeros came to Mexico to live, and brought with them European civilization, has served to endow several generations of Mexicans with feelings of inferiority. Although Mexicans were in New Mexico in 1593, long before there were settlements in New England and Virginia, there was little pride from this historical fact passed

down to Mexican-Indians. The Spanish tradition
with its splendor and romance, its fine horses,
soft colorful clothes and brave men: Juxta posed
with the Mexican tradition of docility, respect
for his father, mother, for God and the church did
not leave a choice for young Mexican people. They
were forced to outwardly respect the Mexican
tradition but their inward thoughts were guided
by the myths, tales, songs that were told of the
Spanish fighting men and their great deeds.

Probably the most damaging element of folklore to the Hispanic people is the lack of heroes
from the lower classes. There are very few
examples of poor Mexicans pulling themselves up
by their bootstraps. Heroes from the lower classes
were not idolized and talked about. Most of the
Spanish people that came to Mexico were from the
upper classes. They came to get richer and to
add prestige to their family names. Education was
not important, competition and change were nonexistent. Families lived as they always had, they
were locked into an economic strata with little
need for literacy. There were no books or newspapers or schools in the early days. Instead of
stories of intellectual achievement, young Mexicans were told stories of Cortez, the God with the
white face, or stories of the Spanish Conquista-
dores. Folklore of this type produced a people
that it was easy to stereotype as being indiffer-
ent, uncooperative, and not caring about education.

Hispanics do not have in their folklore, a
Gutenberg, Galton, or Galileo, they have no intellectual hero of the stature of Comenius, Cleisthe-
nes or Clemnceau. Young Hispanics grew up with
stories of fighters, therefore, their image is
that of Machismo. Instead of relating to books
and schools, young Hispanic men are anxious to
prove that they are "real men". Each young boy
wants to be the boss, if this means he has to
fight he is ready. His father's father was a
fighter, and so will his son become a fighter.
His father was the absolute head of the family

and he intends to become the head of a family.

In the past, there was great resentment of schools among Hispanics. This resentment was caused by a combination of things: first, the past history of Mexico and the United States has been one of conflict. Mexicans perceived Anglos as invaders, braggarts and racists, and the stories that were passed down from generation to generation emphasized these stereotypes. Hispanics also believed that Anglo school teachers looked down on their Mexican background as a mark of inferiority. It has been difficult to separate these myths from reality. In recent years Hispanics have begun to accept the exploits of low income Hispanics as part of their folklore. They are also more receptive to the value of an education. As more and more success stories are told about educated successful Hispanics, and young Hispanic boys and girls are able to lose their sense of guilt because they want to be different from their parents, high dropout rates will go down and school achievement will go up. Lack of motivation, student apathy and non-competiveness will disappear.

CHINESE AMERICAN FOLKLORE

Folklore in the Chinese American community is perhaps stronger, and has had a more significant impact on Chinese Americans than has the folklore of any other ethnic group. American middle class teachers are generally pleased with Chinese American children. When compared with middle class white American children, Chinese American youngsters are perceived as being better behaved, obedient and self-reliant. The Chinese Americans like their Asian counterparts, the Japanese, take full advantage of educational offerings and rank as one of the highest educated of minority groups. (Kitano 1974)

Confucianism, a kind of Chinese philosophical folklore, has dominated Chinese thought for more

than twenty-five centuries. Confucius stressed
human relationships--every man in his proper
place and with his proper responsibilities and
duties. Hsum Tzu revered the teaching of Confucius. Since Hsum Tzu's teachings are now firmly
embedded in Chinese folklore a passage from the
Hsum Tzu is worth quoting:

> Li (rites) rest on three bases: Heaven
> and earth, which are the sources of life;
> ancestors, who are the source of govern-
> ment. Without heaven and earth where
> would life come from? Without ancestors,
> where would the offspring come from?
> Without sovereigns and teachers, where
> would government come from? If any of
> the three had been lacking, there would
> be no men or no peace. Therefore, accord-
> ing to the rites, man must pay homage to
> heaven above and earth below, worship
> ancestors, and honor sovereigns and teach-
> ers. Herein lies the threefold basis of
> ritualism. (Chai and Chai 1962)

With thoughts like those from Hsum Tzu passed
down from generation to generation via the spoken
word it is not surprising that Chinese Americans
were able to survive the harsh treatment they
received in their early days in this country.
This ethnic group had a solid history and a strong
folklore to sustain them. The stories that were
told to young Chinese emphasized ancestor worship,
duty and obligation, filial piety, and importance
of family name. There is a continuity in family
control and discipline, obedience to parents is
central, children are to obey parental wishes,
stay by them, and provide a source of pride and
comfort. (Kitano 1974)

Schools in America have not been a source of
discomfort for Chinese American children; they
have been conditioned by their folklore to conform
to those standards of behavior that are highly
prized by middle class teachers. Chinese children

are quiet, interested in school, hard working
and respectful to teachers. They are as they
are because they have listened to stories of
their Chinese ancestors who lived a "good life"
because they followed these tenets.

NATIVE AMERICAN FOLKLORE

Folklore has held an unique place in the past
and contemporary lives of Native Americans.
Native American is probably the best name that
can be used to identify a group of people who are
the only true natives in America. This group of
people are certainly not Indians, as a lost
explorer called them, and as Europeans who followed him continued to designate them. The correct
way to identify Native Americans would be: Pawnee,
Seminole, Navajo, etcetera. For they are separate
peoples, with separate languages, cultures and
nations. Native Americans of one nation were as
different from Native Americans of another nation
as Italians are from Swedes, Hungarians from the
Irish, or the English from the Spanish.
(Heinrich 1977)

The Native American because of relatively
isolated rural conditions retained a fierce
pride in their ancestoral cultures and group
identity; folklore, in a very special oral
tradition, was and still is used to keep intact
indigenous cultural factors. (Gordon 1974)
There are two examples of Native American folklore that have implications for education today.
Native Americans have been told since the early
1400s about their native ancestors' lives before
Europeans came to this vast continent. They
know from their folklore that the different
nations were highly developed; that society was
jointly held; they had an agriculture system, and
they spun and wove. (Koning 1976)

Most Native Americans would still prefer the
type of life style that they learned from their
folklore, they are philosophically in tune with

86

a tranquil existence. They do not like the "hustle bustle" of urban life, and they are not concerned with the fierce competition required to live the so called "good life." American schools are geared to and supportive of the mainstream society; they are not attractive places for Native American young people. The dropout rate for Native American high school students is perhaps 35%. (Bureau of Indian Affairs 1977) A study of Native American folklore by middle class teachers, along with proper modification of their classes, may lower this dropout rate and increase the pool of talented young people in America.

This brief sketch on American folklore revealed the need for additional study by America's teachers. Many teachers go into multiethnic/ multicultural classrooms and are rudely awakened to the reality that they have been short changed educationally. A knowledge of American folklore will promote a better understanding of the motivation of culturally different children. If teachers know the stories that ethnic groups have been told and the folk heroes that they idolize, they can use that knowledge to break away from middle class American values and learn to appreciate culturally different values. Over the years, many myths, much fiction, and much stereotyping have developed within middle class white society about minorities. A study of the folklore of each minority ethnic group in America will remove the cumulative negative perceptions about culturally different people and make it easier for teachers to modify their behavior, and attitudes and contribute better to the emotional and intellectual growth of culturally different students.

REFERENCES

Blassingame, John W. The Slave Community, Oxford University Press, Inc., New York, 1979.

Chai, Ch'u and Chai, Winberg. The Changing Society of China, The New American Library of World Literature, Inc., New York, 1962.

Fishel, Leslie and Quarles, Benjamin. The Negro American, A Documentary History, Scotts Foresman and Co., Glenview, 1967.

Gordon, Milton M. Assimilation in American Life, Oxford University Press, New York, 1974.

Hamilton, Charles V. The Black Preacher in America, William Morrow and Co., Inc., New York, 1972.

Heinrich, June S. "Native Americans: What Not to Teach," in Unlearning "Indian" Stereotypes, Council on Interracial Books for Children, Inc., New York, 1977

Kitano, Harry H.L. Race Relations, Prentice-Hall, Inc., Englewood Cliffs, 1974.

Klotman, Phyllis R. Humanities Through the Black Experience, Kendall/Hunt Publishing Co., Dubuque, 1977.

Koning, Hans. His Enterprise, Monthly Review Press, Columbus, 1976.

Moore, Robert B. and Hirschfelder, Arlene. Unlearning "Indian" Stereotypes, Council on Interracial Books for Children, Inc., New York, 1977.

Rose, Willie Lee. A Documentary History of Slavery in North America, Oxford University Press, Inc., New York, 1976.

Sowell, Thomas. American Ethnic Groups, Urban Institute, 1978.

CHAPTER 5

CULTURAL AWARENESS: INTERACTION OF TEACHERS, PARENTS AND STUDENTS

George N. Wallace

Educators are now required (and have been for several years) to pay more attention to the cultural differences that learners take to school with them.[1] Diversity is considered to be healthy and schools are being asked to recognize differences and build upon them as strengths. More specifically, teachers are being challenged to turn the anxiety of being different into the pride of being oneself and enjoying others who are unique.

Multicultural education is simply good, diagnostic, and prescriptive or individualized teaching. Educators from William James and John Dewey to contemporary figures like J. McVicker Hunt (1978) have spoken of the "problem of the match" as being the most critical element in education. The "match" means starting or teaching at a point just beyond where the learner already is and preferably in a natural environment. How, then, do we present material with just the right amount of incongruity, familiar but not entirely, new but only in part? Educational psychology has shown that teachers need to begin with and build upon the particular surroundings, experiences, interests, and intrinsic motivations of their students as much as possible, while at the same time interpreting such characteristics within the context of particular stages of cognitive, personality, physical, and moral development. In layman's terms: what you learn best is based on what you already know and can do![2]

The teacher's first job, then, is to find out for each student <u>what is known</u> (e.g., culture, language, academic skills), <u>what is possible</u> (e.g., level of development according to Piaget, Kholberg,

Hunt, etc.), and what is important (e.g., home, family, friends, neighborhood, interests, projects). Such determinations require active involvement and research by teachers into a variety of cultures different from their own. One of the most effective means for gaining this kind of information is through the process of "cultural diagnosis," that is, the process of determining accurately the characteristics of a particular culture.

The central purpose of this chapter is to enable teachers to diagnose cultural differences in a way that will avoid stereotyping and misjudging the differences actually represented by learners (a kind of well-intentioned prejudice or prejudgment that assumes differences where there are none and that overlooks those that are present) and to utilize diverse cultural information to increase their teaching effectiveness.

MAKING A CULTURAL DIAGNOSIS

Culture may be defined as "the learned, shared and symbolic patterns of thinking, feeling, believing and behaving (doing) upon which we rely for security and survival   (Johnson 1977, p. 10). We can assume, up to a point, that these patterns are known for a Gypsy, a Chicano student, a Black student, a cowgirl, or a student from an upper-class Anglo suburb--but such assumptions can be misleading if one wishes to go beyond the stereotypes, as all true educators must. A person's culture is often undescribable since, in its truest form, it is manifest in a setting of uncalculated reciprocity and unconscious belonging. It is, in fact, where and how a person lives right now--where s/he chooses to frequent willingly, and what s/he chooses to do there. When young, most of these patterns are established as guided learning from people sociologists call "significant others," people such as parents, godparents, extended family, neighbors, and after a certain age, peers and adults whom a person chooses to esteem and model himself or herself after.

To find out more than the superficial images and cultural stereotypes presented to us through radio, TV, movies, books, and jokes, we need to become familiar with the specific surroundings and activities of our students in the extra-school setting.

THE SOCIETAL CURRICULUM

Dr. Carlos Cortes (1979) reminds us that schools do not provide the only education. In reality, two curricula operate side by side: the school curriculum and what Cortes calls the "societal curriculum." He defines the societal curriculum as, "the massive, ongoing informal curriculum of family, peer groups, neighborhoods, mass media and other socializing forces that "educate' us throughout our lives" (Cortes 1979). This constitutes most of what we know and have experienced. If professional educators do not construct the school curriculum to complement and extend this less contrived and longer-lived societal curriculum, they may be kidding themselves concerning the staying power of what they teach.

The societal curriculum includes those "facts" that have influence because they are taught by the people and surroundings to which one is primarily bonded or from which one gets long-term security in the form of love, food, shelter, clothing, discipline, protection, and identity. As stated before, the immediate environment seems to have a pervasive influence because it is uncalculated and reciprocal and, unlike school, it is with a person for a lifetime. These influences are not entirely accessible to a teacher since their basis is bio-social. They are described by sociologists and psychologists, however, as the strongest sources of motivation for learning and behaving in a certain way and as the most fundamental basis for social cohesion

91

(Moore 1976).

Home visits are the teacher's best tool for understanding this bio-social level of the societal curriculum. When you know the articles, personal space, names of personalities, family members, smells, and shades of color and light that surround a person, a whole new perspective on that person opens up and you can greatly increase your teaching potential.

> Karl's dad was crippled in a tractor accident, but it never occurred to me that Karl would be living in a trailer on two acres. When he told me he lived in the country and talked about his prize lambs I had pictured a big farm. He dressed the part and obviously was a friend of the other boys whose parents were farmers and ranchers. Now I knew that in order to keep those hopes alive, I must build carefully on their (Karl and his dad's) well-tended sheep project crowded carefully onto that small acreage.[3]

Intrinsically motivated bonding (like that between Karl and his friends) on this level of the societal curriculum accounts for its strength. It involves matters of task and "myth" that are the basis for self concept, identity (Cheek and Burch 1976), and eventually culture if left to operate long enough.

A second level of the societal curriculum involves that part of ones culture that is shared by various social groups which may not be of a primary nature or have a bio-social basis. This includes television, radio, movies, sporting events, magazines, and other such "curricula" that may alter the way students see themselves, depending on the strength and pervasiveness of their primary bonds, and that certainly affect the way they perceive others. One would suspect that the stage of development would also determine the degree to which this level of the societal curriculum temporarily influences ones culture, self concept, and view of other cultures. Children in the concrete operational stage of thinking, for example, are very literal and interpret any media presentation as being "the way it is" (Furth 1970). Cortes reports that "In one study white children said TV comedies like "Sanford and Son" and "The Jeffersons" accurately portrayed Black family life, even when they admitted that such shows contrasted with personal experiences with their own Black friends. They thought their friends were exceptions" (Furth 1970). During adolescence when the pattern of development is to reach beyond the immediate family and neighborhood and expand ones identity, the images and role models in the media seem mysteriously powerful.

Cultural diagnosis involves identifying the heroes and the influential images in the lives of learners as well as the factual and everyday surroundings. The most meaningful interpretation of your students' immediate surroundings (the cultural diagnosis) can be accomplished through visits to the neighborhoods where your students live--through observation of both the physical and social environments, the societal curriculum, affecting your students outside of the classroom.

NEIGHBORHOOD VISITS

When you were growing up, did you have your own routes, paths, hiding and meeting places? What kept you out or in, and who were the people and what was the stuff of your neighborhood that interested you most? What small events do you remember, and what was the setting? It's hard for teachers to get back to the child's view of the world and to focus in on all the ineffable things that are really important to children or adolescents. It helps to experience and to think about the places that children and all learners inhabit of their own free will after departure from the institutional surroundings in which most teachers meet and work with them.

Knowing a student's neighborhood allows a teacher to provide a wider and more interrelated view of those things that a learner will experience over and over again. Simultaneously, the teacher can elevate that which has already been personalized to something worthy of study. This begins to break down the cultural gaps and to narrow the distance between home and school.

Take a walk or a drive through your students' neighborhoods and look for two things: (1) all those things you suspect may be familiar to them, and (2) how you might use those things, along with your own broader understanding, to expand what the child already knows.

He knows where all the poles and wires run--you know which are telephone and which are electrical service.

She knows that path goes down to the river--you know about gravel deposits and flood plains.

They have a stone wall around their yard--you know that the rock is native limestone and you could reveal the drama of its undersea formation.

A large cottonwood tree has dominated a particular vacant lot for 20 years. Every kid there has climbed it, been inside the tree house, and swung from its rope. It is dying and has a large variety of fungi, insect life, and decay. Rather than studying bacterial cultures with a laboratory recipe, you ask two students to bring decaying tree tissue from the old giant. (If they ever cut it down you intend to use a cross section of the trunk as the framework for a social studies unit on local history.)

Determine the characteristics of the neighborhood by sharpening your own powers of observation and analysis. Look first at the specific physical surroundings. (The physical surroundings are easier for most teachers to use when first involving the students' cultures in the classroom.) Note such things as:

stairways, ramps, ladders
roofs, arbors, eves, soffits
fences, trellises, banisters,
    boundaries
doors, windows, grates, cellars
architectural styles, additions,
    ages of things
lot size, shape, layout
walks, paths, streets, alleys
gardens, decor, animals
workshops, garages, out buildings
cracks, ditches, gulleys (they
    absorb countless children)
people in the streets and what
    they are doing
junk, refuse, stockpiles, waste,
    resourcefulness
systems of support, water, power
    sewage, mail, drainage, fire,
    police
furniture, rugs, pictures, adornment
lighting, study and play space,
    space per capita
animals, pets, projects
signs of religious affiliation,
    icons
collections, "customizing,"
    decorations
music, art, posters, toys,
    games
foods, utensils
gathering places, landmarks
ages and makes of cars, decals,
    bumper stickers

The social characteristics are less visible
and must be learned about over time, involving
much interaction with the students and their
families. Knowledge of the physical environment
can later be combined with a knowledge of the
social environment, separating the two less and
less once familiar with the neighborhood. The
social environment would include such things as:

> roots, origins, geographical ties
> distribution of age groups
> family roles, sex roles, authority
> preferred radio stations, movies
> language, dialects, intonation, pitch
> jokes, dinner hours
> schedules, employment patterns
> relatives, extended family, godparents
> names, naming
> gestures, posture
> activity, pastimes
> values, myths
> beliefs, attitudes, customs and
>   traditions

You can be very effective, however, with
knowledge only of the physical environment. If,
for example, you know there is a Catholic church
in the middle of the neighborhood and that most
kids go to Mass, you don't have to understand the
Mass or the relationship of Guadalupe, the Mexican Madonna, to the Virgin Mary, but you can
acknowledge their existence by simply alluding to
both or either incidentally while explaining a
vocabulary word like "ceremonial" or "symbolic"
or while talking about the history of the West,
missions, development of agriculture, or architectural styles. The point is that tying into and
building onto what is already known yields high
educational gain and is a way of subtly showing
respect for the background and lifestyle of every
student.

By now you are thinking it may be a good idea
to spend time making some home visits, walking in

new neighborhoods, analyzing TV shows, or in other ways finding out about what happens in the lives of your students beyond the school. But is it practical? In many cases it can be, and for some more than others. The teachers who have done it and knew what they were looking for are almost unanimous in their opinion that it has worked for them. Three case studies written by teachers describing their neighborhood visits are included at the end of this chapter. One reports on an eye-opening after school walk with two students, and the other describes one teacher's efforts to incorporate her neighborhood observations into a classroom unit. The third case study involved a walk in an urban center.

The bulk of this chapter has centered on neighborhood analysis since teachers have identified it as the most practical and useful tool for doing any diagnosis of culture and for finding characteristics of the immediate environment to use in class. If you have a self-contained classroom with 30 students, it is entirely feasible to conduct a cultural diagnosis, especially if it is a neighborhood school or a school where the neighborhoods that kids come from are distinctive (most are). If your students are bused to school, it is easy and effective to ride the bus once in awhile; not only do you get the complete tour, but you often learn where particular kids live and which ones are neighbors. There is no uneasy feeling about driving around and gawking and it is an excellent first reconnaissance. If you are a secondary teacher who sees 100 kids a day, you may wish to focus on just one neighborhood that is not as familiar to you--perhaps one that has typically been considered a "disadvantaged neighborhood."

Home visits may not be feasible for all your students, but if you plan to teach in an area for awhile, two walks and five home visits every six months will eventually add up to a lot of useful information. Much information can be picked up

vicariously on your way to and from places--if
you take the time to look. Attending church,
coaching little league, or other activities outside the school setting and within neighborhoods
are also excellent ways to learn about your
students' cultures and to win the support of
parents and community.

"DISADVANTAGED" NEIGHBORHOODS

Much has been written about the "culturally
disadvantaged" student and, although the term
"disadvantaged" has been replaced in some places
with the word "different," a certain imagery of
the barrio, the "slum," the reservation, or "what
it's like across the tracks" still prevails.
"Disadvantaged" neighborhoods have always been
considered detrimental to a person's education or
upbringing because the physical and social surroundings were "deprived" of whatever it is we
consider to be good for young people. Nobody was
ever very specific about what it was that caused
this deplorable situation except to occasionally
generalize that kids didn't get good nutrition,
enough sleep, there weren't enough books around,
the TV was always blaring, people used poor grammar, and things were generally junky and run-
down--no place to raise a child. It has long
been considered the job of the schools to "com-
pensate" for that deprived environment by providing a rich and stimulating one at school.[4]

It is this author's contention after several
years of studying neighborhoods that, with few
exceptions, "disadvantaged" neighborhoods can be
as rich and stimulating as any other neighborhood and are often more interesting. Since many
teachers were not brought up in low income or
ethnically different neighborhoods, they may not
have a good idea of what is there and, consequently, may not know how to use or build on those
things at school. It is, therefore, important to
take the time to analyze "different" surroundings
and to remember that the criteria for a rich and

stimulating environment include the following
(White and Watts 1974)[5]:

- how much diversity is there in the
  visual field?
- how much access does one have to those
  phenomena?
- what kinds of new information are
  potentially available?
- how many sources help to reveal that
  information?

Several years of neighborhood analysis have
revealed that low income areas or neighborhoods
typically labeled as "poor environments" tend to
have:

- buildings with a wide range of ages,
  additions, and variety of personalizing
  features (colors, outbuildings, fences,
  yards, decorations), etc.
- people with a wide range of ages (old
  people, those usually institutionalized
  at higher income levels)
- more cottage industries (locksmiths,
  hairdressers, corner groceries, handymen,
  seamstresses)
- less conformity (gardens in the front
  yard, homemade sculptures, lot layout,
  landscaping, trim)
- more landmarks, history, visible change
  and evolution (vacant lots, abandoned
  houses, converted buildings)
- mature vegetation, trees
- animal projects (goats, rabbits, calves,
  chickens)
- hiding and gathering places (shortcuts,
  odd or leftover areas, marginal land,
  swamp)
- discarded materials good for tree and
  club houses, toys and inventions (scrap
  lumber, bricks, pipes--brought home by
  blue collar parents)
- things being built or repaired, or torn

99

apart (cars, plumbing, streets, insulation)
- more people out and about (more walking, porch chatting, errands, late hours)
- fewer covenants and restrictions that inhibit the movement of children
- more visual access to "what's going on" in this place or that
- more intercourse between families and young people, movement from one house to another (houses closer, less locking up, bedtime later, extended family)
- fewer organized or institutional pursuits that necessitate going to another part of town by car
- the presence of assorted mini-economies (barter, trade, hand-to hand cash exchange)
- more machines and apparatus that are manual in nature or where the principal of operation is evident (clotheslines depending on evaporation, can openers with exposed gears, uncles tearing their cars apart, chickens being butchered in the alley)
- more support systems are visible to the eye (telephone and electrical are above ground, sewers steaming beneath manhole covers, newspaper flung to the doorstep) and public transport
- zoning contrasts enable continual viewing of business, industry, manufacturing, railroads, airports, waste treatment plants--which are more apt to be nearby
- families tend to be larger and most children have more brothers and sisters to learn from and imitate

One can see tremendous potential for teaching in these neighborhoods. The visual field, the sheer amount of diversity in what a child is exposed to, and the access to everyday phenomena defy the description of "disadvantaged."

THREE NEIGHBORHOOD VISITS
CASE STUDIES IN CULTURAL DIAGNOSIS

The following neighborhood visits were taken
by teachers as a means to relate more closely to
their students. These teachers were participants
in a workshop on cultural and linguistic differences.

A Neighborhood Walk

By Orville and Sarah Hays

We made our walk in the Denver Five Points
area on Saturday, June 16, 1979. The Five Points
area is a noted Black and Chicano neighborhood
where the general public is fearful to go (whether
or not that feeling is justified or imaginary).

When given the assignment we were hesitant
about walking in that area. Sarah mentioned the
assignment to a Black friend here on campus who
said she had a friend who had an office in the
Five Points area and that he would take us on a
walk. We contacted this man who is Black and a
doctor and he said he would be glad to take us on
a walk, and we made an appointment for 3:00 p.m.

We parked in the Juvenile Hall lot and walked
to his office about a block away. On the way
we met two young Black men who seemed to be
questioning why we were there and we had an
uneasy feeling about it.

The doctor took a great interest in our
being interested in the area and spent a considerable amount of time explaining the make up of
the area, the progress being made to update the
community, and the Five Points Business Association which is leading the program for progress.
Our one hour walk turned into a 2 1/2 hour survey
and briefing on the area. We were introduced to
the leading citizens of the community who seemed
pleased to have us visit them and invited us back.

101

We think this introduction is necessary
because it gave our walk a different perspective
and it gave us a different feeling about the area,
a different attitude. The people seemed like any
other people. However, if Sarah had not made
arrangements with the doctor we probably wouldn't
have gone, or it would have been an entirely
different walk. I'm sure it would have been
shorter and we would have missed a lot.

Observations:

People - All Black except one Chicano
lady and a white couple who
owned a store.
Most were unfriendly until
introduced by the doctor.
Most people were well-dressed.
In one block people were loitering
in front of stores, but most
people on the street were going
someplace.
There was one child, a few teen-
agers, some in their twenties
and most were 40-80. Almost no
people visible in the residential
area.

A general observation about the community was that
of two pictures: (1) homes and buildings were
well-kept, painted, and landscaped, and (2) homes
and buildings were run-down, not painted, trash
lying around, run over with weeds, broken windows,
boarded up windows, screens missing or torn, and
wood was deteriorating. In general it was a low
income area.

Building An abandoned coach factory in
bad shape, a building converted
to a church in good shape, a
fairly new well-kept apartment
house and not far away a fairly
new run-down, vandalized apartment building, a neighborhood

health center converted from a bakery (this is a government project and the first one established) a new modern building that will be the new home of the neighborhood health center, Mitchell Elementary School in excellent condition (this is a feed-in school for upper middle class children for racial balance).

Homes   The architecture is that of tract homes of the early 20th century. They are small, close together, small lots, a porch in front, many with iron fences around the lots. A number of the houses were vacant and run-down. There were some empty lots. Most homes were very old and made of brick. One was a frame house that must have dated back before the fire (about 1886). A few porches had old couches on them but most had nothing. Two or three people were sitting out on the porches, but in general few people were visible in the residential section. The sidewalks were all the original flagstone walks and in good shape. Outside stairways were old and dilapidated.

Industries One, a deep rock water bottling plant with the artesian well still being used.

Stores   Cleaners, cosmetic and modeling studio, numerous bars, pool hall, shoe repair, Churches' Chicken Place, a diner, food market, hotel (with famous Black entertainers), a liquor

103

store, curio shop, hardware store, clothing store, doctor's office, and a gas station being remodeled into a plantation style, old fashioned Bar-B-Que restaurant (by the doctor). One plumbing business (father of Sarah's student).

<u>Cars</u>   Parked on the street, no garages, some wrecks on vacant lots, all types from semi-wrecks to new and from small to new cadillacs.

The business community has an organization called the "Five-Points Businessmens Association". It was organized to upgrade the community, get the people to clean-up, fix-up, paint, etc., and to get the banks in downtown Denver to loan money to the people in the Five-Points area to upgrade the area.

A Neighborhood Walk

By Elaine Elner

Thanks to my students Blake and Bob I know many of <u>the</u> places surrounding Boltz Junior High School that attract the kids for a variety of reasons. The best reason being it's a good place to "hang around"; and besides "all" the other kids hang around there.

We went to places only a junior high student would find to "hang out". We not only looked at fences and ditches but a tree house, a lake, a skating rink, a bar, a tree and a yellow road grader. Most of these gathering places were for the purpose of socializing--smoking and drinking included.

A first look at the new neighborhood reveals many empty fields, new houses, fences, and few trees. It seems so sterile compared to the older

104

neighborhood areas. The older areas and the low income areas do have more things and alleys and junk and places to be or to hide. Most of all, the older neighborhoods have what the kids and I think the most of--trees. Trees are so beautiful and useful; the kids seem to naturally congregate around them. The only tree house we found was one in the middle of the large field behind Steele's (market). This old hideout was abandoned for an old barn that is found near Edora Park. The new hang-out is decorated with old chairs and matt-resses.

A second look at the area, with a student guide revealed many places of interest for the kids to socialize. The following places are the important places to be for many of the kids at Boltz. Of course, there are numerous other places, but the kids picked these as best.

The Bridge

Everyone stops at the bridge on the way to school, during school, and on the way home. Some of the kids do not care who sees them and smoke while leaning on the grate. Most of the kids go under the bridge. They even have some heavy cardboard to sit on. This is a very important place to socialize.

The Grader

Just south of Boltz, behind the new houses, there is an open field and a big yellow road grader (actually a scraper). All of the windows have been broken out by the kids, throwing stones. It is an eyesore, but it is a magnet to the kids. Different social groups are found here: the couples, the smokers, and the climbers. It is a place where you really should not be to do some things you are not supposed to do, i.e. "fun".

The Tree

The Tree, or as it is affectionately called,
"The Smoking Tree" is just a few yards to the
north of the school building, on school grounds.
Last year you could find half the student body
out there smoking at any given time of the day.
In fact, one of the counselors suggested putting
in a phone on the tree so she could get hold of
the kids faster. Unfortunately, someone even
set the tree on fire last year.

This year there are not so many smokers at
the tree due in part to the tightened "no smoking" policy by the Board. But there is still a
carry over from last year and it is still the
smoking tree. It is no doubt a great place to
be, either in or around the tree. Actually, it
is the only tree for acres around that area.

Century Mall Area

A great place to meet is anywhere at the
Century Mall, especially the Red Baron. They've
got all kinds of machines and lots of friendly
faces. In one area of the mall there is a "back
room" that allows the kids alcohol and cigarettes.
Naturally this is the big time to those who enjoy
smokes and liquor. Not everyone hangs out here
in the "back room" but everyone does meet some-
where around the Mall.

Royal Gas Station

This gas station at the corner of Swallow
and College Avenues is where many of the kids
stop to socialize, to buy candy and gum, and to
buy cigarettes. It attracts all the area bike
riders since it is an oasis for goodies and air
for bike tires.

Warren Lake

Warren Lake is about a half mile southeast
of the school. There is also a baseball diamond
and bleachers. The barbed wire fence that used
to be around the shore is all tangled up with
some logs and bushes. The kids say it is a great
place to be, especially in the spring. There are
trees to climb, a lake to fall into, and a lot
of walking room. The kids feel that this area
is very relaxing.

Roller Skating Rink

All the kids go to the roller rink. There
are some interesting ditches between the railroad
tracks and the rink that are just lined with cans
and cigarette butts. Bob says that the kids
group around the building and in the ditch. From
what the kids said, as many kids just "hang
around" as those that actually skate.

Neighborhoods of the Students

Around O'Dea School there is a rickety fence,
while a nice fence surrounds Parkwood's swimming pool and houses. There is also a difference
in kinds of houses found in Parkwood as compared
to those across from O'Dea. The kids are sensitive to where they live and the cost of the
houses, but it does not keep some of them from
running together at school.

On the other side of the area is Imperial
Estates. Most of the houses have fenced-in
horse pastures.

There are many fences in the area surrounding the school, built to either keep people out
or to stake out territory. The fences next to
the Bridge, are to keep people (kids) out of the
swimming pool and off the tennis courts. In the
neighborhood a little north of Boltz, the neighbors are fiery mad because of poor planning and

impossible fences. There is no way to get from
one yard to the other without going around the
block, and each yard has a different type of
fence.

Tennis Courts and Smoke House

To the northeast of the school there is a
historic site--the smoke house--and the private
tennis courts. The sign in front of the smoke
house offers a reward to report anyone seen near
the building. The kids do not go near there for
fear of getting into trouble. The sign at the
tennis courts says "Private" and the gate is
locked--not very receptive. The kids really stay
away from the inside of both.

Undoubtably, you have noticed how many times
the expression "hang around" was used in describing the kids' activities. That was the most
common reason they gave me for their activities.
The kids really enjoyed just being with (hanging
around) each other whether it was talking, walking, smoking, or sitting.

I immensely enjoyed the walks with the kids,
they were quite enlightening. They gave me a
chance to see the area in which they live and
to see what the kids do outside of school.
Furthermore, I was delighted at the initiative
shown and with the willingness to help me when
I asked them.

Note: Many teachers report that the newer
tract home developments have fewer kids actually
doing things in the neighborhood, or even visible
on the streets. One could speculate that until
a neighborhood "matures" it has little appeal.
Puberty is, of course, time to begin "breaking
away" and carving out ones individuality and
simultaneously pleasing ones peers. Some cultures
in some neighborhoods seem to allow this to happen

closer to home.

Teaching with Old Tires

By Nate Archuleta

When I went down to Old Town to talk to some Chicano kids about coming to school for today's micro-teaching, I noticed about seven of them playing with old tires. Another boy was watching a neighbor change a tire. I decided to do something in class with tires. Tires are part of the kids' every day environment; tires lay in most vacant lots, along the river and in many of their back yards. "Tireness" is something already in their minds; it is something to plug into and to see if we can get a little extra mileage out of.

How does one prepare for something like this? Well, you stand ready to go in a number of directions for one thing, because, while you may plan on a number of concepts and kinds of language, it can always go in an entirely new direction, or not go anywhere at all. Here are some things that might go through one's mind in planning a lesson around the kids' environment:

Words that might be modeled to label, explain, compare, speculate:

tread	alignment	blowout
groove	balance	tube
studs	circumference	straight
steering	mileage	tubeless
traction	worn	nylon
wheel	out of line	punctured
rim	synthetic	slicks
sidewall	vertical	

Words that could be expressed in Spanish:

direción	neumático
perforado o punturado	ranuras o muescas

109

aro   llanta
goma

Specific questions one could ask if the cues were
presented:

> What kinds of tires do the "low riders"
> (A chicano sub-culture) prefer?
> What kinds of tires do you have on your car?
> Why do they make different kinds of tires?
> How do you change a tire?
> How do tires wear out?
> Why do you suppose this tire is worn on this
> side only?
> How can we tell if the tires are still good
> or not?

CONCLUSIONS

It is necessary, of course, to look for the
characteristics of <u>all</u> students' neighborhoods,
rich or poor, rural or suburban, blue collar or
professional, inner city or horseman acres, Chicano or Irish. The culture of any group can be
found in their surroundings and, after all, we are
talking about multicultural education.

It wouldn't be accurate to surmise that this
is all there is to cultural or even neighborhood
diagnosis. A gread deal of information flows in
and out of all neighborhoods from mass culture
and is constantly being assimilated and accommo-
dated--it changes and it is changed. Teachers
can, however, increase their effectiveness in
educating all students, especially those students
having cultures different from their own, by
becoming more culturally aware through the process
of cultural diagnosis, by analyzing the societal
curriculum and by visiting their students'
neighborhoods.

REFERENCES

Cheek and Burch. The Social Organization of Leisure. New York, Harper and Row, 1976, Chaps. 1, 6, 87 and the afterward.

Cortes, Carlos. "The Societal Curriculum and the School Curriculum: Allies or Antagonists" in Educational Leadership, April 1979, p. 475-480.

Furth, Hans G. Piaget for Teachers. Prentice Hall, 1970.

Hunt, J. McVicker. "Stimulus Variety," in Educational Psychology - Selected Readings, Sprinthall & Sprinthall, eds. Addison Wesly Publisher, 1978, p. 99-101.

Johnson, Norris Brock. "On the Relationship of Anthropology to Multicultural Teaching & Learning" Journal of Teacher Ed., Vol. XXVII, June, 1977.

Moore, Wilbert E. in The Social Organization of Leisure, Cheek & Burch, eds. Harper & Row, New York, 1976, Introduction and pp. 76-82.

FOOTNOTES

1. National Council for Accreditation of Teacher Education Standards, Jan. 1979.

2. Stressed, by Dr. Marie Hughes in a lecture at the University of New Mexico, October,1970.

3. From a conversation with a Vo-Ag teacher in Fort Collins, Colorado, 1976.

4. Title I of the Elementary and Secondary Education Act.

5. Burton White and Jean Carew Watts, report in Experience and Environment, Prentice Hall, 1974. (There are no formal criteria for measuring the amount of interaction, richness of stimuli, or access to stimuli, but the authors do suggest what these criteria should be.)

CHAPTER 6

COUNSELING THE CULTURALLY
DIFFERENT STUDENT

Vivian L. Kerr

Counseling is a discipline of considerable
importance in satisfying the culturally different
student's basic needs for security, love and
belonging, esteem and pride, and self-actualization or self-development. In order to assist
culturally different students in meeting their
basic needs, counselors must be prepared to
communicate "humanistic qualities of maturity,
mental health, and effective interpersonal relations." In order to be effective the counselor
must also be able to accept the culturally different, to be genuine, and to respect the client.
The counselor must also be able to convey the
characteristics of spontaneity, self-disclosure
and concreteness.

There is a current controversy concerning
whether a middle class white counselor can
effectively counsel culturally different clients.
Although the situation might not prove to be best
and problems may occur, it is the opinion of the
writer that with the proper training, preparation,
and qualities, a middle class white counselor can
effectively counsel culturally different clients.

Counseling Minority Students

Counselors of today are becoming aware of the
need for the counseling of minority individuals
and their own lack of experience and preparation
to meet those needs. Most counselor's required
curriculum includes no subject matter dealing with
ethnic minority groups. Little research has been
conducted in the past to provide adequate and
comprehensive textbooks concerning culturally
different/ethnic minority clients. Therefore, any
information received by students has been in the

form of bits and pieces presented by guest
lecturers and/or special readings or assigned
individual projects included in traditional courses by concerned professors. In such cases,
however, the student still does not, and should
not, feel competent to adequately help an ethnic
minority client.

.   There are several issues concerning counseling that cut across all three of the areas of
counseling covered in this paper: racial attitudes, testing, staffing, language, and client
readiness and expectations. The issues are important and relevant to each counselor who works with
culturally different clients. A knowledge of the
issues and assumptions can make a counselor more
sensitive to his/her own feelings, attitudes and
prejudices and provide a stronger base for an
initial interview with the ethnic minority client.

Racial Attitudes

Racial attitudes in the counseling experience
are not solely considered from the counselor's
perspective. Clients also have racial attitudes,
positive or negative, concerning the counselor.
All people have preconceived ideas about people of
different backgrounds based on stereotypes and/or
personal experience. Quite often people generalize their feelings and/or ideas about one individual to encompass an entire group of people.

Counselors who see that the value systems,
dress, achievement, and motivation of minority
clients are different from their own might be
repulsed or angry. The hostile minority client
who is demanding and aggressive, or sullen and
non-communicative may cause the counselor to feel
alienated and unable to help the client. Even the
counselor who begins with good intentions and a
positive attitude might feel overwhelmed and
resign him/herself to the futility of the effort.

The other side of the problem is the client.

The client might have anti-Anglo feelings based on previous experiences. Grier and Cobbs (1968) term this is "racial paranoia". Frequently the minority client blames his/her present living conditions on all Anglo people. Thus, the client feels that the Anglo counselor cannot help him/her with his/her problem because the counselor, by being Anglo, in a sense is part of the problem.

The professional counselor must be prepared to deal with the negativism of the minority client. He/she must deal with these feelings if a meaningful relationship is to exist. Therefore, it is important that the counselor deal with his/her own personal bias concerning ethnic minority individuals prior to the counseling situation.

Testing

For many years, the area of testing has been a controversial topic when related to ethnic minority group members. Standardized tests are recognized by contemporary professionals in the appropriate areas as being culturally biased. However, the recognition of the biased nature of tests has not eliminated their use or resulted in the provision of bias free tests, if such instruments were possible.

Measurement is an important aspect of many phases of life. It is important to have a variety of activities in order to have additional perspectives from which to make decisions. Still, test results should be viewed as no more than one component of an individual's total self.

The issue involved in the testing of ethnic minority individuals is not the score itself, but rather how the score is used or misused. The counselor cannot rely on the results of tests to predict the future success of an ethnic minority individual. The counselor must use other sources to evaluate the ability and potential of the ethnic minority client.

Staffing

Staffing problems exist in almost every setting in which a counselor will be employed. In most cases understaffing is the rule rather than the exception. It is difficult in this type of situation to provide the quality of counseling for each client that is necessary. For ethnic minority clients the effect of understaffing can be most harmful.

The minority client, who has little understanding of the counseling process and negative feelings concerning the counselor, requires more time than an individual who is at a higher level of awareness. If the time is not provided, some of the negative feelings may be reinforced and the client lost forever.

There is a limited number of minorities employed as professional counselors. "As is true in almost every profession, minorities are under-represented within the ranks of professional counselors. In part, of course, this is simply the result of racism in the United States." (Hoyt and Valdez 1975) Another reason for the under-representation at the present time is the educational requirement of a Master's Degree. Many minority youth cannot afford the additional time required to continue school beyond the baccalaureate level. Now, however, many minority teachers and social workers who are furthering their educations are choosing counseling. This perhaps is due to a recognition of the needs of minority youth to receive adequate counseling in the schools.

Communication is the foundation of counseling relationships. The counselor expects the client to be able to express his/her feelings and thoughts to the counselor. Communication in standard English may be a difficult task for ethnic minority clients.

For these clients slang and non-verbal
communication are important means of expression.
In order for the individual to survive and
communicate within his/her environment, he/she
must understand and speak the coded language. The
problem in the counseling relationship lies in the
emphasis placed on the use of language by the
counselor. If accurate empathy is important, it
is important for a client to choose a helper who
is likely to understand him. A counselor who
shares the client's socioeconomic, educational,
and other background variables is likely to
understand the client more thoroughly than a helper who is quite distant from the client on these
variables. Therefore, if a client has a choice
of two high-level helpers, he would do best,
generally, to choose the helper whose situation
is closest to his. (Egan 1975)

However, the counselor must avoid using
language that is not comfortable to him/her in
an attempt to identify with the client. Generally,
this tends to alienate the client rather than make
him/her comfortable. It is read as phony, and
the counselor loses the trust of the client.
Genuineness is an important aspect of the communication process. The counselor must be genuine
enough to say, "I don't understand what that
means."

Client Readiness and Expectations

Another issue relevant to the effective
counseling of an ethnic minority client is the
client's readiness and expectations. In many
cases the counseling experience is new to the
minority client. His/her expectations of the
counseling situation and/or the counselor might
be different from the majority group client. The
minority client is also often an unwilling client.

Quite often the minority client is referred
to a counselor by another agency or individual.
In those cases the client is referred for

117

corrective measures. The counselor might be the last stop before suspension, prison, loss of children, etc. Thus, the client associates the counselor with a possible negative action.

The client also often views the counselor as an authority figure. He equates the counselor with the principal, policeman, social worker, doctor, or lawyer. The minority client's experiences with other authority figures might have been negative and dictatorial. Therefore, by associating the counselor's role with that of other authority figures, the client might expect the counselor to tell him/her what to do.

The minority client, due to past experiences and lack of understanding of the counseling process, enters the counseling relationship with negative expectations and little preparation. The counselor has to assume an attitude of goodwill toward the client to get him/her involved in the learning process. Respect for the minority client means that the counselor communicates to his/her client a deep and genuine caring for her as a person with potentialities, a caring uncontaminated by her thoughts, feelings, or behaviors. (Rogers, 1967)

In the initial stages of the counseling relationship, the counselor must help the client define the role of the counselor and client. The counselor must assist the client in the acquisition of certain skills conducive to the relationship. The counselor must also begin the relationship at the level or readiness of the client and assist the client in increasing his/her level of awareness and readiness.

Educational Counseling

A major responsibility of the counselor working with ethnic minority clients is to provide adequate educational counseling. Historically, minority students from low-income backgrounds

118

have graduated from high schools and schools of higher education in disproportionately small numbers. With the current job market demanding qualified people with an expertise of specialized training in specific areas, the unemployment rate for ethnic minorities who are undereducated remains high. One aspect of the solution to underemployment and unemployment is to encourage ethnic minority group members to be prepared academically to attain their career goals.

The counselor can play a major role in the endeavor to attract minority group members into non-traditional programs of study. The counselor can encourage these individuals to attend and complete school and stimulate their academic achievements toward higher levels of education.

In order to adequately provide the assistance needed by minority group members, it is important that the counselor be aware of the issues and needs of the individuals in relation to the educational system. Although the concerns, needs, and problems are basically the same for the different age groups and educational levels, some are more appropriate for specific levels.

ISSUES AND NEEDS

Educational Aspirations

Many highly talented low-income and minority students do not aspire to the levels of educational attainment of which they are capable. The following are a few of the numerous causes for the absence of aspiration: (a) the lack of previous encouragement; (b) the feeling that a university education is inaccessible for various reasons; or (c) the feeling that they would be unwelcome, since so few of their peers have preceded them. Therefore, it is important to maintain personalized practices early in the student's academic career.

Financial Resources to Meet Expenses

The most common characteristic of minority
students is their lack of financial resources.
Any delay in obtaining funds, any miscalculation
of eligibility, any change of financial status,
any nonappropriate funds from outside agencies,
or any unexpected emergency can bring havoc to
the scholastic efforts of the student. It is
essential, therefore, that counselors remain
current in all areas of financial aid programs
available to students. Moreover, in the case of
the high school or elementary school counselor,
intervention by the counselor after high school
graduation on the part of the student might eliminate any possible problems as a result of financial dilemma.

Academic Skills

Some minority students enter high school or
post secondary school with skill deficiencies
which render them at a disadvantage when competing
with other students. These skill deficiencies
are not a sign of a student's inability to succeed
at the particular school. Rather, they are an
indictment against the elementary schools, high
schools, and community colleges which the student
attended prior to entering the particular school.
Therefore, the counselor must work in conjunction
with the various support service programs to
supplement the student's previous education.

Educational and Career Decisions

Few minority students have solid plans when
they leave high school and/or enter post secondary
schools. The uncertainty of career and post
graduate opportunities may have a counter-produc-
tive effect on the student's academic progress--
some students consider it reason enough to drop
out. Therefore, to create a positive focus for
the total educational experience, there is a need
to provide career and graduate school counseling.

Personal Adjustment

Most minority students have experienced educators' rejection and disparaging comments regarding their ability and potential. Because these students have been told for so long that they are "educationally deprived" and "culturally disadvantaged," they may possess acute feelings of inadequacy. Therefore, there is a need to provide sensitive and quality professional and peer counseling services.

Family and Domestic Readjustment

Depending upon a student's background and age, the role of a student has varied ramifications. For a young student leaving home to attend a post-secondary school for the first time, problems of family and community loyalty, suspicion of the school, and parents' reluctance to have children influenced by other values are prevalent. For the married student there is often a change of roles. In cases of couples with children, the problems are obvious--enough money for self and family support, finding suitable child-care facilities, arranging school and work schedules so that the child is cared for at all times. Therefore, there is a need to involve family members in the transition of minority students to institutions of higher education. Hopefully, their involvement will generate support and encouragement for the entering students.

Adjustment to the Higher Education Systems

The process of adjusting to an institution of higher education involves learning to function within a higher bureaucratic organization. This includes understanding the rules, regulations, and procedures of the school, (e.g. enrollment, registration, course selection, petitions for adding and dropping courses, and departmental and university requirements for graduation). Unless students are properly trained, counseled, and

periodically advised in these procedures, they
will become confused, frustrated, discouraged,
and may eventually leave.

In order to meet the educational needs of
the student, the counselor needs to establish
goals and objectives that are realistic for
his/her setting. The goals and objectives will
be different, of course, depending on the type of
school or agency he/she works out of. An example
of a list of goals and objectives that can be
incorporated into a counseling program to facili-
tate the ethnic minority client is listed below.

General Goals of Educational Counseling

1. To assist incoming minority students
    in facilitating their personal,
    social, and academic interaction
    with the school environment.

2. To assist minority students in making
    the transition from high school to
    post secondary school life.

3. To increase the likelihood of survival
    in the school system for minority
    students beyond the age of sixteen.

4. To develop an appreciation and accept-
    ance throughout the school for the
    contributions and potential contribu-
    tions minority students can make to
    the growth and development of the
    school.

5. To continue to develop and strengthen
    a positive rapport between the minority
    student and the total educational
    community.

6. To assist in the recruitment of minority
    professionals.

122

7. To promote cohesiveness by acting as a basis for unity among all students.

8. To continue to work toward the acceptance of the minority student as a positive aspect of the school by the total educational community.

Specific Objectives

1. To assess incoming students' strengths and weaknesses and to help each individual know where to go initially to receive support for his/her deficiencies and outlets for his/her strengths.

2. To improve the efficiency of minority students in relation to organizing their time for effective study.

3. To improve the efficiency of minority students in organizing information to be processed from textbooks and lectures.

4. To help minority students grow increasingly sensitive to how their personal needs, academic attitudes, and goals relate to the resources and opportunities in the educational community.

5. To help minority students set realistic goals and develop useful strategies for attaining these goals.

6. To encourage minority students to support and participate in activities and programs that are sponsored by other groups in the school.

7. To begin to develop skill and openness in small group discussions with the ultimate goal being to enhance communication experiences for minority and

majority students.

8. To help minority students develop
   initially realistic and beneficial
   relationships with teachers.

University systems have recently recognized
the problems and needs of the culturally different
student and have instituted special programs to
meet those needs. Special needs programs are
designed to provide academic support services to
ethnic minority and low-income students. Although
the programs vary throughout the country in size
and financial support, most attempt to provide
counseling, tutorial assistance, and ethnic
programming. The main goal is to make it easier
for culturally different students to remain in
high school and to ease the transition from high
school to a college, university, or other post
secondary institution; and in a majority white
school, cushion the "cultural shock" that may
occur.

REFERENCES

Carkhuff, Robert R., The Art of Helping, U.S.A., Human Resource Development Press, Inc., 1973.

Egan, Gerard, The Skilled Helper--A Model for Helping and Interpersonal Relating, Monterey, CA, Brooks/Cole Publishing Company, 1975.

Grier, W.H. and Cobbs, Price M. Black Rage, New York: Basci Books, 1968.

Rogers, C.R. and Truax, C.B. The Therapeutic Conditions to Change: A Theoretical View. In C.R. Rogers (Ed.) The Therapeutic Relationship and its Impact. Madison: The University of Wisconsin Press, 1967.

PART III

TEACHING STRATEGIES FOR CROSS-CULTURAL SETTINGS

CHAPTER 7

ASSESSMENT OF MULTIETHNIC/MULTICULTURAL STUDENTS

IN CROSS-CULTURAL SETTINGS

William E. Sims

The "fair testing" component of Public Law
94-142 requires that testing and assessment
methods be comprehensive and fair--that is, testing must be nondiscriminatory and cannot be based
on a single criterion or index such as the I.Q.
score. The "fair testing" component should be
used in educational settings for children including those not specified in the nation's most
comprehensive legislation dealing with special
children--the Education for All Handicapped
Children Act. Teachers working in crosscultural
schools (schools that enroll Anglo-Americans,
Black Americans, Hispanic Americans, Native Americans, and Asian Americans) should make every
effort to adopt the "fair testing" procedure for
their classes. Differences in cultural values
among ethnic groups require a variety of assessment procedures.

Teachers using traditional assessment methods
(those suited for middle-class white students)
with culturally different students will cause
frustration for their students and themselves.
Most of the discipline problems encountered in
multicultural schools are the result of utilizing
improper assessment techniques. Culturally
different children have been deeply hurt by the
insistence of middle-class teachers that they
conform to middle-class academic standards that
many of them cannot meet. Since they are culturally lacking in many skills required to "pass
the tests" they rebel and become discipline
problems and in some instances destructive
vandals. This point cannot be stressed strongly
enough; middle-class teachers, sometimes without
malice, radiate to culturally different children

127

the feeling that if you cannot "pass the test" you are inferior and do not belong here. This feeling of worthlessness creates intense hostility in culturally different children and they vent their feelings in the only way they believe is left open to them. Much of the destruction in schools and most of the physical abuse inflicted on teachers can be eliminated if teachers and schools will give serious consideration to changing their assessment procedures.

Teachers are now required to complete courses in educational psychology and they know that reward is more effective, as a motivational device, than punishment, but for some unknown reason the majority of teachers still use tests to discipline and scare students; this is a fundamental problem in the educational process for culturally different students. High anxiety makes learning difficult, and drives students away from public education. Nothing in the academic environment produces more anxiety than tests. Innovative teacher education programs must prepare teachers to use a variety of assessment techniques to lower anxiety in culturally different students.

Teachers for the eighties in schools with an increasing number of culturally different students, are challenged to select assessment techniques that are best suited to the students, all of the students, that they will serve and the instructional outcomes they seek.

MEASUREMENT, EVALUATION, AND ASSESSMENT

The three terms--measurement, evaluation, and assessment are often used by teachers interchangeably; for the purposes of this discussion some distinctions will be made between these terms. "Measurement" is inclusive and implies abstracting information about students through observation, rating scales, and other testing instruments. Measurement is concerned with the gathering of data through the use of tests and

128

scales. Teachers derive numerical scores from these instruments to assess student behavior in all academic subjects. Measurement scores reflect students' achievement. (Travers 1979) Evaluation depends largely on the results of objective, standardized tests that have been carefully prepared in order to make them both precise and valid. (Lindgren 1980) Evaluation also includes informal and intuitive judgements about pupil progress, as well as the act of "valuing" or identifying what kind of behavior is desirable and good. (Thorndike and Hagen 1977) Assessment is a process of observation or measurement very similar to evaluation, but does not always involve value judgements as clearly as does evaluation. (Savin 1969)

Assessment is a better teaching technique than evaluation for culturally different students. It is easier for such students to relate to observation because it is less threatening than evaluation and observation does not require value judgements by the teacher. It is difficult for the culturally different student to understand and appreciate evaluation components that requires the acceptance of specific values and the use of a variety of tests as the basis for teacher value judgements.

The overriding concern of both assessment and evaluation is to enhance instruction and to improve learning. A secondary concern of both is to provide motivation and direction. Traditional teachers, however, often use evaluation for a variety of reasons other than those higher purposes. Teachers all too frequently use tests to restore order in the classroom or to punish students for poor academic performance.

The problem with traditional evaluation techniques centers in the longtime search by traditional teachers for what they call "treating all children equally." Traditional teachers want all students to conform to middle-class

American standards,to have similar views on education, to read the same books, to find the same
things humorous or sad, and to enjoy the same
food, music, art, and drama. Then they can give
students the same types of objective tests to
determine the degree to which educational goals
are being reached. Far too many teachers believe
that all students should be measured in the same
manner; to them evaluation that is fair and equal
involves the acceptance of specific values--
middle-class American values. Culturally different children do not bring to the school the same
experiences as middle-class white children;
their experiences are somewhat unique. Because
of the life long uniqueness of each culturally
different group, it can be seen that each group
will perceive academic situations differently.

Traditional teachers have been fairly
successful with the use of evaluation to discipline middle-class white students, because
middle-class white students are receptive to
academic discipline; they are exposed to this
type of discipline in their home environment.
Middle-class children are often told, "if you
don't do your homework you cannot have dessert"
or "if you read this book you may go to the
movies." Reward and punishment are intimately
tied to academic activities. Therefore, middle-
class, white students will respond positively to
the use of evaluation that is negatively used.
Such is not the case with culturally different
students.

THE CULTURALLY DIFFERENT STUDENT

Culturally different children, because of
the pressures within their environment, face a
more practical world. They have a different
perspective on reward and punishment. Culturally
different children are not generally rewarded for
academic accomplishments, and they are not pun-
ished for poor performance; rewards are given for
more tangible accomplishments,and punishment,

generally for misconduct. A culturally different
student may feel that school attendance is punishment and that skipping school is rewarding. It is
difficult for a traditional teacher to understand
a culturally different child that has little or
no respect for education. It is unsettling for
these teachers to hear a child who is racially
or culturally different say "I don't like taking
tests", or "I don't care if I fail this test."
It is unwise to assume that students with these
feelings will do well on tests.

Culturally different students are not
concerned with conforming; they, therefore, make
it difficult for middle-class white teachers to
understand them. Middle-class American teachers
are not prepared for culturally different students, wearing "far out" clothes, acting differently from middle-class children, believing in
ethnic things, expressing themselves emphatical-
ly, using street speech. Teachers and students
are caught in a cultural dilemma that is not
conducive to academic development.

Culturally different children, generally,
are more easily taught and evaluated by teachers
who understand that for them learning is an
emotional experience. They learn through doing,
feeling, and thinking, just as middle-class
children do, but the order is not the same. A
middle-class student will learn by direct
involvement, followed by a thinking process,
and finally feeling may be brought into play.
Involvement and thinking are more important to
these students. If they feel anything about the
situation, it comes after the "doing" and
"thinking". A good example of this middle-class
trait can be demonstrated by this question asked
by middle-class parents of their children. They
ask them "What do you think of this?" For most
culturally different children the most important
consideration is how they feel about a learning
situation. If they feel positively about the
teacher-learner situation, they will get involved

131

and the thinking aspect will follow. An example
of this culturally different trait can be inferred
from the way a question may be posed by culturally
different parents. They ask their children, "How
do you feel about this?"

APPROPRIATE ASSESSMENT AND ATTITUDE

What can a traditional teacher do to ease
the academic problems of culturally different
students? First, they must realize that standardized tests are usually culturally biased, and
culturally biased tests will not produce a fair
evaluation of a culturally different student.
Secondly, if a school district insists on using
standardized tests, the teacher should devote
time to prepare the culturally different child
for those tests. The teacher can also emphasize
in his/her teaching material the information
found on standardized tests. An important focus
of teaching in a multicultural setting should be
preparation of the culturally different child
for academic testing. It is better to have
culturally different students experience test
anxiety than to surprise them by administering a
test with insufficient lead-time. Teachers should
also keep and share with students and parents
an accurate record of the students' assessment
during the year. Culturally different students
must always have a clear understanding of how
they are progressing. If the above suggestions
are followed, the culturally different student
will show steady improvement in his/her ability
to take a test. Even this small success will
give the students confidence and make it easier
for the teacher to prepare them for testing.

If a culturally different student does not
feel good about an academic situation, especially
a stressful situation such as evaluation, his/her
participation will be half-hearted at best. In
cases like that, direct observation is the best
procedure to follow in obtaining data. What the
student says or does not say, what she or he does

132

or does not do can be observed and inferences made about his/her true feelings. Teachers should use direct observation to get feedback from culturally different students on results of academic activities. It is not necessary to develop a test and require written completion to obtain feedback on instruction.

It is a human trait to avoid any task that will lead to failure. This is true for any person; it is especially true for culturally different children in academic settings. Most culturally different children are not prepared by their culture for the middle-class emphasis on testing; therefore, they face all measurement activities with trepidation. They actually believe they are going to fail.

TEACHER ATTITUDES AND EXPECTATIONS

Culturally different students do not need a discouraging classroom setting where the teacher is impersonal and authoritative; they need teachers who are willing to use different assessment tools and innovative teaching methods. Teachers need to develop skills in assessment, through observation rather than through testing. Teachers should give culturally different students academic tasks that are challenging, but that also have built-in success assured. Culturally different students also need teachers who believe in their potential. Students believe what teachers tell them even if they pretend not to. A teacher who is farsighted enough to provide encouragement to culturally different students can make a real difference in their lives. If the teacher believes in the child's potential, eventually the child will learn to believe in his/her own ability. When students believe their teacher has respect for their ability, in spite of past shortcomings, they can face academic obstacles with greater confidence.

The most powerful incentive students can

133

have is the belief that their teacher believes they have ability. With this type of understanding, students feel they can do anything that is required of them and do it with merit. All teachers should be aware of the success stories of culturally different students who have been rejected by public schools and middle-class teachers. These are stories of successful people who were, in a sense, "tested out" of the public school system and then reclaimed by sensitive, nonjudgemental teachers, who did not "look down" on people. Such stories would not have merit if the number of cases was small, but there are thousands of these cases. It must be stated that these success stories are not found in the literature, and they are not common knowledge among teacher educators, but they are true, there are many, and soon they will be brought to everyone's attention.

The television program "Sixty Minutes" has already brought Marva Collins to the attention of America, and traditional teachers have been explaining away her success ever since the program was beamed into their family rooms. They can't believe that an unassuming, highly articulate, Black, former Chicago public school teacher can take the rejects from the Chicago public schools and teach them to read, understand and appreciate the classics, and to work, easily, higher mathematics. These ghetto born and reared Black students have IQ test scores too low, according to their middle-class counselors, for them to master these intellectual tasks and are supposed to be genetically handicapped for high status components of western culture. Be that as it may, these students perform above the national norm in the basic skills and they read and enjoy Shakespeare, Milton, Plato, and Tolstoi; they write poetry and music, and they are as at ease with the sciences as they are with the arts.

Some of the public schools in Brooklyn, New York, because of culturally aware administrators

and concerned, understanding teachers are
upsetting the measurement prediction and educating Hispanic students above the predictions of
their test scores. Visit the multicultural
schools in Los Angeles, Washington D.C., and
Atlanta and you will find that culturally different children can succeed when teaching is good
and evaluation is fair.

SUMMARY

Public Law 94-142 contains a fair testing
component that assures parents and students that
testing and assessment methods will be compre-
nensive and fair. This Act, however, was written
and made law for the protection of handicapped
children, thereby protecting them from discriminatory testing and placement in special classes
based on single criterion or index such as an IQ
score. The same type of protection, to the letter
of the law, should be used to protect culturally
different children. It is a fact of life in
education that standardized tests are used to
predict how well a student may perform in school.
It is also common knowledge in education that
test results of minority students are used to
place them in special classes, on slow tracks or
noncollege preparatory classes. All of these
occurrences influence the lifetime progress and
success of culturally different children.

The most damaging result of standardized
tests is the effect that they may have on middle-
class teachers who are receptive to the idea that
tests are infallible. Test results for these
teachers may lead to a self-fulfilling prophecy,
whereby teacher expectations based on test scores
become confirmed by student performance.
(Rosenthal and Jacobson 1968) It has been and
probably will continue to be a practice of teachers to praise and relate positively to students
with high IQ scores. This extra attention serves
to enhance the students' achievement. The
students with low IQ scores on the other hand

are generally neglected especially if they are minority students. These students are not given the extra attention that they need and they fail just as the IQ conscious teacher expected them to. Teachers seem to forget that if a culturally different child scores low on a standardized test because of the inadequacy of his/her environment, it is not the test which is unfair, but the social order which permits the child to develop under such conditions. (Mettrens 1969) Furthermore, if a teacher knows that a child is culturally different and yet interprets his/her scores as if the situational appropriateness of these tests were valid, then the child is receiving poor quality teaching as well as unfair evaluation.

REFERENCES

Block, N.J. and Dworkin, Gerald. The IQ Controversy, Pantheon Books/Random House, New York,
NY, 1967.

Lindgren, Henry Clay. Educational Psychology in
the Classroom, Oxford University Press, New
York, NY, 1980.

Mettrens, William. "Standardized Test: Are They
Worth the Cost?", Education Digest, Sept. 1976.

Rosenthal, Robert and Jacobson, Lenora. Pygmalion
in the Classroom, Holt, Rinehart, and Winston,
Inc., New York, NY, 1968.

Savin, Enoch I. Evaluation and the Work of a
Teacher, Wadsworth Publishing Company, Inc.,
Belmont, CA, 1969.

Thorndike, R.L. and Hagen, E. Measurement and
Evaluation in Psychology and Education, Wiley,
New York, NY, 1977.

Traver, John F. Educational Psychology, Harper
and Row, New York, NY, 1979.

CHAPTER 8

DEVELOPING POSITIVE MULTIETHNIC/MULTICULTURAL

LEARNING ENVIRONMENTS

Howard Bruner

Culturally different youth are a subject of growing interest among teachers across the country. The problem of teaching the culturally different child exists in urban and rural America alike. How does the teaching style or technique differ in effectively reaching culturally different ("disadvantaged") children? According to Jack R. Frymier, . . . studies clearly support the notion that youngsters who come from disadvantaged backgrounds have less positive motivation to learn in schools than youngsters who come from advantaged backgrounds. Many federally sponsored projects were designed specifically to come to grips with this phenomenon. The fact that not all those projects have been dramatic successes should not cause us to give up--the problem still exists. Motivation is inextricably intertwined with the socio-economic situation, and somehow, some way we must get hold of that problem more effectively than we have to date. (Frymier 1970)

It is a fact that culturally different children are influenced differently by motivational factors. These factors might not be important except that teachers frequently deal with youngsters in the classroom as if they were all the same: one class, one method, one experience for all students. Persons whose motivations are different have very different kinds of self esteem, attitudes, values, goal orientation, time perspectives and personality structures.

It will be the object of this chapter to provide a practical knowledge and application of motivational principles that can have a positive influence on the culturally different

139

student.

MOTIVATION: THE KEY TO EFFECTIVE LEARNING

Motivation is the strongest force in all human behavior. It is the force that impels a person to behave in a certain way; it influences everything an individual does--choices, priorities and decisions. Motivation is the power behind all individual actions.

The force that is so important in daily human behavior is equally important for the classroom teacher. Motivation is a teacher's first problem, one that is dealt with not only at the outset of learning, but one that must be maintained at an optimal degree throughout the teaching-learning process. There are two major challenges, for the teacher to motivate himself/ herself. The greatest motivational force yet discovered is a highly motivated teacher. Often what is thought to be a highly motivated class is, in actuality, a highly motivated teacher whose enthusiasm and interest are caught by the class. (Douglas 1968) The second challenge is to motivate the students in the classroom under the jurisdiction of the teacher. For the sake of clarification it should be stated that the only true mode of motivation comes from within and is referred to as "intrinsic motivation." In order to stimulate the learner, however, extrinsic motivational strategies become an extremely important part of the teacher's responsibilities. Much of what is discussed in this chapter concerns external strategies that must be planned by the teacher. The awakening and development in students of positive motives and a strong sense of purpose is the most valuable service a teacher can render.

MOTIVATIONAL THEORY

Although any number of motivational theories might be described, the practical suggestions

provided here relate most closely to Abraham
Maslow's "Hierarchy of Needs Pyramid" and Frederick Herzerg's "Two-factor Theory of Motivation".

Maslow saw human needs falling into a ladder
hierarchy. (Frymier 1970) He suggested that
needs gratification is the most important single
principle underlying all human behavior. His
pyramid proposes the hierarchy of needs: placing
psychological needs at the bottom, progressing
through safety needs, acceptance needs, self-
esteem needs, the need for self-actualization, the
desire to know and to understand, and at the apex
of the pyramid is placed aesthetic needs.

Biehler makes a case for the practicality
and usefulness of Maslow's theory for teachers:

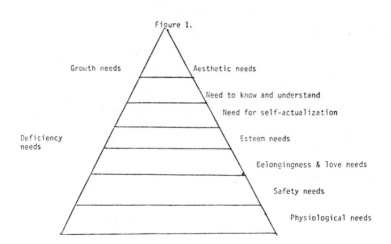

Figure 1.

Growth needs

Aesthetic needs

Need to know and understand

Need for self-actualization

Deficiency
needs

Esteem needs

Belongingness & love needs

Safety needs

Physiological needs

141

The implications for teaching Maslow's theory of motivation are provocative. One down-to-earth implication is that teachers should do everything possible to see that the lower-level needs of students are satisfied so that they are more likely to function at higher levels. Your students are more likely to be primed to seek satisfactions of the need to understand and know in your classes if they are physically comfortable, feel safe and relaxed, have a sense of belonging, and experience self esteem.

Teachers using Maslow's hierarchy find themselves in an ideal position for guiding their students toward satisfying deficiency needs prior to seeking growth needs gratification.

Frederick Herzberg, from the University of Utah, extended and refined Maslow's concepts on needs satisfaction by developing the "Two-factor Theory of Motivation." He established support for two relatively independent factors: (1) obstacles or "dissatisfiers" to needs satisfaction; and (2) providers of needs satisfaction. Herzberg described these two factors in the following ways.

"Dissatisfiers" (obstacles) to needs satisfaction:

1. Poor interpersonal relations with teachers or school administrators

2. Poor interpersonal relations with peers

3. Inadequate instructional assistance

4. Poor school rules, regulations and policies

5. Poor classroom learning conditions

6. Personal problems of students
   (outside school)

Providers of needs satisfaction:

1. Achievement

2. Recognition

3. Satisfaction in school work itself

4. Responsibility

5. Advancement-promotion

Herzberg's studies indicate that high motivation and production is closely related to job satisfaction and rewarding work. These essential ingredients sound very much like Maslow's emphasis on acceptance and esteem needs.

CHARACTERISTICS OF LOWLY MOTIVATED STUDENTS

Student failures and dropouts may seem to be so apparent to the teacher that such a classification may not be necessary. The model characteristics, however, may provide some clues on how to work with poorly motivated students. The following characteristics were developed by William W. Farquar in his studies on motivation and academic achievement.

1. Immediate versus long-term gratification.

The lowly-motivated student desires short-results. He has little tolerance for abstract, delayed rewards.

2. Common versus unique accomplishments.

The lowly-motivated student has a standard of achievement that is more peer conscious than teacher conscious. He wants to do what his friends do and often has

143

negative feelings about academic accomplishments that make him stand out from the crowd.

3. <u>Ease of competition versus meeting a standard of excellence.</u>

The lowly-motivated student appraises school standards on the basis of where the cut-off point is for "getting by" and does not view them as a challenge for excellence. His attitudes are realistically tied to his devaluing the standards, because they stand for little more than irritation or obvious failure.

4. <u>Low versus high job or school task involvement.</u>

The student with low academic motivation indicates little desire to invest himself in learning activities, whether school or future-job oriented.

5. <u>Negative versus positive self concepts as a learner.</u>

The lowly-motivated student feels that teachers would most likely use negative words such as "stubborn, lazy, uninterested, or distractible" to describe him. In short s/he has a poor self concept as a learner.

6. <u>Low level of academic compulsiveness.</u>

The lowly-motivated student feels little need to complete tasks just for the sake of completing them. What is more, s/he fails to display the appropriate guilt for not having finished the task. Neatness, orderliness and punctuality are not valued for their own sake.

7. High level fantasizing.

    Students who have little motivation to
do school tasks indulge in much fantasizing
to escape reality. For boys, the daydreams
are highly sexual in nature and are often
triggered by a momentary stimulus. For
girls, the daydreams are a release from
unpleasantness--a retreat to a place where
people are happy and life is interesting
and fun.

8. Low impulse control.

    Poor impulse control, whether in the
form of anger or out of the need for
excitement, is a frequent problem associated
with the female who is low in academic
motivation.

9. Hostility toward authority.

    The male who has low academic motivation
has feelings of anger against those who
direct his school existence. His anger is
related to his being told what and when to
do something; it is often unrelated to the
reasonableness of the order.

10. Aimlessness.

    The lowly-motivated male feels a perva-
sive lack of direction or purpose. He
either has no goals or considers them
unimportant. (Rudman 1968)

The previous list of characteristics,
describing the lowly-motivated student, is not
intended to provide for the teacher a comprehensive and absolute guide for identifying students
that need special assistance in developing
interest in school work. More importantly, the
list suggests special needs that appear to be
significant in striving to relate effectively to

the culturally different student--implying that all culturally different students are lowly-motivated.

DEVELOPING MOTIVATIONAL STRATEGIES

Of all the many responsibilities assigned to the teacher, by far the most important is the teacher's ability to stimulate learning and to create an inner desire on the part of the student to want to learn. Through the teacher's own behavior and the selection and application of proper methods and techniques, he or she has the capacity to dramatically promote or impede learning. The teacher and the teaching process can make the difference in the student's acquisition of new knowledge, developing new interests and attitudes, or mastering new skills.

There is no one set formula, strategy, or special set of techniques that will motivate all students in just the same way or to the same degree. What turns one student on may not work with others. Don Hamechek suggests:

> If we can begin by agreeing that motivation to learn is a complex blend of different environments, attitudes, aspirations and self-concepts, then we are a step closer to effectively using what research tells us about how to improve both our teaching and learning practices.
> (Hamachek 1979)

THE ASSUMPTIONS OF THE TEACHING-LEARNING PROCESS

The following assumptions regarding the teaching-learning process are made:

1. The activities of teaching and learning are closely interrelated with the results in one being highly dependent on the other.

2. Teaching is the process of professional

146

decision making and the translation of those decisions into actions makes learning more efficient, stimulating, and purposeful.

3. Constraints within the individual or his/her environment can be minimized by appropriate teaching decisions.

4. Teaching decisions and actions are subject to control. These actions yield a powerful and predictable influence on learning; but learning itself is not under the teacher's control.

5. Motivational principles can be translated into action as the teacher interacts with students.

THE PRINCIPLES OF MOTIVATION

Students can be stimulated to learn using the basic principles of motivation. The teacher may, through application of these principles in classroom activities and proper application of interpersonal relations, encourage students to want to learn. The following principles are most appropriate for students with different cultural orientation and backgrounds and should provide some guidelines for arousing and sustaining their interest in school.

1.   Physiological Needs as Motivators

Teachers should be aware that students function best in seeking needs satisfactions when the learning environment is physically comfortable. The physical drives such as thirst, hunger, and exhaustion are primary motivators that must be satisfied before functioning at higher levels. Concurrent with the physical needs mentioned are the concerns for safety and health conditions.

The following suggestions can help

147

the teacher in satisfying physiological and safety needs of his/her students:

   a. Strive to provide for students who may need nourishment by serving lunch or snacks.

   b. Make a thorough safety check of facilities used by students while participating in curricular and cocurricular activities.

   c. Cooperate with the home in caring for students who became ill while attending school.

   d. Strive to make the classroom physically comfortable (e.g., room temperature, air circulation).

   e. Provide rest and relaxation periods when students have been involved in intensive and extensive physical or mental activity.

2. <u>Emphasizing Purpose Enhances Motivation</u>

   If a student senses a practical purpose in an educational experience, the individual pursues the activity with more zest and enthusiasm. It is a well-known concept that when a person develops goals which s/he sees as personal, the learning process is stimulated. Helping students perceive goal identification and purpose is a primary responsibility for the teacher. For example, a purpose motivator common to most youth about sixteen years of age is the desire to want to drive. With this goal orientation the student can be urged to read extensively in textbooks and manuals on driving. Likewise, if a student wishes to improve interpersonal skills with the opposite sex, the individual may be motivated to become proficient in in dancing.

Teachers may have difficulty in helping students relate to long-term goals. Most young people, and particularly culturally different youngsters, are stimulated most effectively by identifying short-term goals.

The following can aid the teacher in helping students develop a sense of purpose:

a. Help students identify goals that are personally attainable. Frustration caused by tasks that are unreasonable and out of reach for the student may deter.

b. Stress goals that are student choices rather than dictates of the teacher.

c. Plan for goals that incorporate immediate rather than long-range satisfaction particularly when working with students with low motivation. An example would be to plan a party for the class once it has succeeded at a rather difficult task.

d. Intended goals and purposes should be clearly understood by the teacher prior to the teaching-learning experience.

Hoover summarizes this point well:

People normally regulate their actions to achieve desired ends. Imposed tasks that merely keep people busy are avoided whenever possible. Not only should purposes be known, but they should be interpreted in terms of everyday problems of those involved. (Hoover 1964)

3. Active Involvement and Motivation

"Students learn by doing" is a phrase frequently used by teachers to illustrate how they feel about the importance of involving students directly in educational experiences. Students' interests in school tasks can be stimulated and they can be encouraged to participate and to become involved through direct, real experiences. These firsthand activities provide the foundation for some of the richest, most stimulating, motivational practices.

Dale's cone of experience vividly portrays the progression of learning experiences ranging from direct, purposeful participation to purely abstract student involvement. (Figure 2, Dale 1950) The base of the cone represents the concrete, firsthand experiences through which the student is provided a rich variety of sensory stimulation. This practical, direct activity assists immeasurably in the internal processing of information. When rich, active learning is achieved, there is a notable increase in the amount of learning and length of retention.

Generally verbal, abstract methods are not suitable for the academically low-motivated student; the teacher should always search for concrete, tangible ways of involving students.

The following suggestions can help the teacher in planning active student involvement:

a. Utilize the community as a laboratory for learning. Take the students on visits to places where they can participate directly in a firsthand learning task.

150

b. Physical activities are very useful
    in classes with culturally different
    students. Acting out scenes or role
    playing can sometimes be very effec-
    tive since many times these students
    are physically oriented.

c. Use the students' cultural back-
    ground for practical suggestions for
    direct involvement. Special activi-
    ties centered around such things as
    music, dance, holidays, games and
    costumes can actively involve the
    student and at the same time develop
    respect for his/her culture.

d. Compile a comprehensive list of
    culturally oriented resource people
    that can come to the classroom and
    stimulate interest in classroom
    tasks.

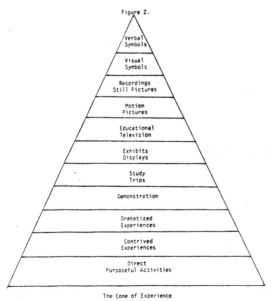

Figure 2.

Verbal
Symbols

Visual
Symbols

Recordings
Still Pictures

Motion
Pictures

Educational
Television

Exhibits
Displays

Study
Trips

Demonstration

Dramatized
Experiences

Contrived
Experiences

Direct
Purposeful Activities

The Cone of Experience

151

4. Rewards as Motivators

Advocates of modification urge teachers make extensive use of reward in order to provide feedback for positive reinforcement. If a teacher wishes to encourage participation and elicit good behavior, some kind of material reward system can be a useful incentive. Several important ideas to keep in mind in understanding rewards and student behavior follow:

a. Positive reinforcement is more effective than negative reinforcement. Having one's errors pointed out is less effective than telling a person that they are doing something right.

b. The reinforcement-reward should be provided immediately after the satisfactory behavior in order to be most effective.

c. When a student engages in an activity primarily because s/he will earn recognition or reward from the teacher, it is called intrinsic motivation.

d. The teacher should make it a practice of commenting favorably on successful performance and avoid calling attention to failure.

e. The teacher should assist the student in transferring external reward to intrinsic motives (self-gratification).

f. When using reward incentives the teacher should have a variety to choose from, selecting rewards suitable to individual needs.

g. Before using a reward system, consider

carefully possible disadvantages
of controlled education.

There is substance to the concept that
learning can be encouraged and sustained by
the appropriate use of rewards. The teacher
should take care, however, that rewards
should be sincere and that students have a
feeling that they have been earned.

5. Being Appreciated is a Strong Motivator

Showing appreciation is a spin-off of
rewards as a procedure for giving positive
feedback to the students. Psychologists note
that one of the strongest human desires is to
want to be appreciated.

If a student is doing commendable work
or does something special above and beyond
the call of duty, the individual should be
recognized by some special gesture of appreciation. Such efforts for commending good
behavior will contribute immeasurably to
high morale and positive attitudes. Appreciation in some form makes students feel
significant, worthy, and needed; without
appreciation displayed in the classroom,
learning will be impaired. Guidelines for
the teacher in showing appreciation:

a. The teacher should recognize that
    assigning grades is neither a
    reward nor an act of appreciation.

b. When possible, show appreciation on
    a personal, one-to-one basis.

c. When appropriate show appreciation
    in public. Make mention of special
    commendation before the entire class.

d. Remember students' names and some-
    thing special about each individual.

e.   Catch students doing good deeds--
     give them a catchy card of recogni-
     tion.

f.   Be aware of your nonverbal behavior.
     Teachers send more messages of
     acceptance or nonacceptance with
     their body language than any other
     way.

Remember, the one difference between
giving rewards and giving appreciation is
that, although both are motivators, appreciation has no strings attached. Only
appreciation can sincerely be given on either
potential or performance. That's why it
simply must be among a teacher's repertoire
of human relations skills. (DeBruyn 1975)

6.   Reach Students with Positive Attitudes

The effective teacher understands that
being positive is a state of mind. It is a
mental outlook toward life and for teaching,
it is attained with a strong desire to
believe in people and always to look for the
possible instead of the impossible. Having
a positive attitude carries with it a desire
for being constructive and productive. The
positive teachers find themselves issuing
many "do's," "possible's," and "let's try."
On the other hand, negative attitudes are
disruptive, destructive, and nonproductive.
The negative teacher is observed issuing
"don'ts," "can'ts," "impossible's." It is
important to keep in mind an important law
of human behavior, that in the absence of
positive attitudes, negative ones are most
likely to take over.

The outstanding teacher fully understands
the importance of positive attitudes as a
strategy for motivating students and realizes
that the teacher is constantly displaying

behaviors that are interpreted as positive
or negative forces.

The teacher can send positive messages
by:

a. Developing a belief in students.
   Students are likely to perform in
   accordance with the teacher's
   expectations.

b. Sending facial gestures and body
   language messages. Indications of
   approval, acceptance or rejection,
   and dissatisfactions are often made
   by a smile, glare, or frown.

c. Confronting negative attitudes
   openly and demonstratively.

d. Encourage students to display positive attitudes and optimism in the
   classroom.

7. Build Motivation on Successes

Success-conditioned students possess
high motivational levels while students with
failure conditioning have low drives for
achievement and learning. Individuals tend
to raise their goals and extend their level
of aspiration after experiencing success.
With this in mind, the teacher should strive
to plan for student successes while avoiding
failure experiences. Students from culturally different backgrounds may frequently
experience failure in the schooling process
rather than success. Their inability to
speak or write the language, the lack of
assistance and support from the home or
isolation from the dominant culture may be
reasons for their difficulties in registering
successes in school. Teachers should be
particularly aware of the troublesome

motivational consequences of a situation in which the individual is bombarded with successive and excessive failure experiences.

In light of the importance of success in stimulating students to learn and grow and the fact that failure frequently depresses it, several suggestions are made as guidelines for teachers' classroom behavior:

a. Plan learning experiences that are challenging but attainable. Fit the school work to the students; make assignments students are capable of doing and from which they can get a sense of accomplishment.

b. Make sure that students have adequate study resources to complete class projects and homework. Frequently, culturally different homes are deficient in periodicals and reference books.

c. Give carefully prepared instructions to students on how to study effectively while completing classroom assignments. Student frustration may grow from vague or unclear directions.

d. Offer a variety of ways for students to achieve success. Classrooms are frequently organized to recognize only the academically-talented students. Provide opportunities for students to display their talents in a variety of ways—drawing, illustrating, acting, dramatizing, serving.

e. Capitalize on existing student interests. Projects and activities

in the classroom centered around
things students like to do are more
likely to enhance student successes.

8. Help Students Improve Their Self-Esteem

One of the strongest motivational forces
is the drive to be accepted and valued by
those around us. People with strong self-
concepts are likely to succeed while students
with weak self-esteem are likely to fail.
Hamachek describes this clearly.
(Hamachek 1979)

> Probably one of the most important
> findings growing out of research dealing
> with the certainty of self-esteem lies
> in the implications for at least inter-
> rupting the vicious cycle whereby low
> self-esteem students confirm their self-
> image by (1) avoiding experiences that
> might otherwise help them view them-
> selves more positively, and (2) disbe-
> lieving their successes when they do
> have them so they can maintain their
> consistency.

Frequently the culturally different
student may have developed a feeling of
inadequacy or have a weak self-image. The
causes may be from any number of events
experienced at home, the neighborhood, or at
school. If the individual has been made to
feel unworthy, incompetent or inadequate by
parents, friends, or teachers, the result is
likely to be a weak self-concept. The
student bombarded by successive failures or
frequent rejections is very likely to be
poorly motivated.

Black self-concept has undergone massive
positive changes in recent years. But the
general impact of Pettigrew's statement still
holds for many minorities in American society.

To be different, whether Black, Indian, Chicano, Jewish, Italian, or Croation, is likely to mean being "less than" the majority group. Consequently, students who belong to a minority group are especially likely to have negative self-concepts in at least some respects. Teachers should be aware of this problem. They should carefully monitor the school environment so that traumatic incidents that can lower self-concepts are minimized.

It is important at this time to respond to the question, "How does one determine self-worth?" A person isn't born with it; it is received from one's environment, from one's family, peers, and teachers. The teacher's role is significant because it is closely tied to the individual's acceptance and success in school activities.

Motivation is so closely related to building student self-esteem that some of the following suggestions may be extensions of previous teacher strategies:

a. Develop a variety of ways to show importance for students' work. Give verbal acknowledgment, send positive nonverbal messages, use students' ideas, exhibit classroom projects, recognize accomplishments before the entire class.

b. Show respect for all cultural groups in the class. Using resource people in class representing cultural minorities is an excellent way for the teacher to show respect.

c. Individualize and differentiate the projects and work to be done by students. Make assigned tasks commensurate with varying abilities and interests that are possessed by

158

the students in the class.

d. Initiate procedures that allow for peer approval to be shared by students in the class. Group activities and cooperative projects can encourage student involvement and recognition.

e. Provide assistance for students in dealing with special classroom frustrations. The teacher can reduce frustrations by helping students with language problems or helping students with study resources.

f. Provide opportunities for students to express themselves. Many students may feel they have lost their identity in large schools and classrooms. Allow students to select projects and activities that relate to their world.

9. The Importance of Enthusiasm

Students in classes can be motivated by an interesting and enthusiastic teacher. Enthusiasm is contagious, and a highly enthusiastic teacher tends to develop highly interested and enthusiastic students. In some instances enthusiastic students can motivate other students.

There are many ways the teacher can instill enthusiasm in the class:

a. The teacher must believe in the importance of the subject s/he is teaching. The teacher must think that the subject has merit and value for each of the students.

b. Verbal behavior of the teacher must be used to effectively enhance the classroom.

c. Nonverbal behavior should be used to effectively encourage the students.

d. Make use of change-of-pace activities in the classroom. The teacher should be especially responsive to the attending behavior of students. If the class appears to be bored or growing weary of the class activity, the teacher should be ready for an alternative activity.

e. A frequent change of appearance in the classroom can communicate enthusiasm. New bulletin board displays, room decorations, and changes in the room furniture can help achieve a new and refreshing look.

BUILDING A MOTIVATION ACTION PLAN

A case has been made for mastering and employing a set of motivational principles in order to help students achieve instructional goals and purposes. Motivation, however, is too important in the teacher-learning process to be left to chance. If a teacher wishes to make improvements in teaching behaviors and strategies, a plan must be developed for implementation. Such a plan should provide a way to assess one's real teaching self and suggest practices for improving the interpersonal relations in the classroom. An outline for a self-improvement plan for motivational behavior is suggested.

I. Prepare a written motivational improvement plan

A. The plan should state objectives to

be achieved

B. The plan will act as your conscience and reminder

C. The plan will help hold you accountable

II. Make visible changes in the classroom environment

A. Provide new study assistance for students

B. Prepare new room decor and display areas

C. Improve communications with parents and the home

III. Develop a reward and recognition system

A. Recognize students for birthdays, illnesses, and special honors

B. Extend recognition of students to faculty, administration, and the home. Give attention to good things being done by students

C. Create or invent your own recognition and reward symbols (cards, prizes, trophies, certificates)

IV. Assess your motivational actions

A. Make video tape of your classroom behavior. View objectively your verbal and nonverbal activity in the class

B. Keep track of the cards and awards you give to students

C. Keep a record of telephone calls and personal conversations you have in showing appreciation and recognition to students

D. Determine your level of openness by keeping a count of all students who come to you with a problem when unsolicited

It is totally within the jurisdiction of the teacher to change the attitudes and atmosphere of the classroom. If a teacher desires to improve the motivational climate in the teaching-learning setting, the effort must be goal oriented and the teacher must visualize purpose or reason in the activity. Pursuance of such a plan over an extended period of time should result in a change in the behavior of the teacher and, consequently, an improvement in the quality of motivation in the students.

REFERENCES

Biehler, Robert F. <u>Psychology Applied to Teach-</u><u>ing</u>, 3rd Ed. Houghton Mifflin Co., Boston, 1978, pp. 517-518.

Dale, Edgar. <u>Audio-visual Methods in Teaching</u>. Holt, Rinehart, Winston, Inc., 1950, p.99.

Debruyn, Robert L. "A Primary Factor in Motivation." <u>The Master Teacher</u>, October 6, 1975, Manhattan, KS.

Douglas, Leonard M. <u>The Secondary Teacher at</u> <u>Work</u>. D.C. Heath, 1968, p.32.

Frymier, Jack R. <u>Motivation Quarterly</u>. Fall 1970

Gage, N.L., Berliner, David. <u>Educational Psychol-</u><u>ogy</u>. Rand McNally College Publishing Co., Chicago, 1975, pp. 411-412.

Hamachek, Don E. <u>Psychology in Teaching Learn-</u><u>ing, and Growth</u>, Allyn and Bacon, Inc., 1979.

Hoover, Kenneth. <u>Learning and Teaching in the</u> <u>Secondary School</u>. Allyn and Bacon, 1964, p. 99.

Rudman, Herbert, Featherstone, Richard. <u>Urban</u> <u>Schooling</u>. Harcourt, Brace and World, 1968, pp. 199-202.

CHAPTER 9

SELECTING EDUCATIONAL MATERIALS FOR THE

MULTICULTURAL[1] CLASSROOM

Bernice Bass de Martínez

One of the most critical elements of a successful instructional program is the selection of program materials. Often emphasis is placed on the curricular goals and objectives with some concern expressed over the implementation of the curriculum. However, unless the materials are carefully and thoughtfully selected in relation to what the implementor and the curricular writers had in mind, the plan is likely not to succeed.

In reviewing the development of a curriculum, one recognizes that five critical components are involved: the needs assessment which identifies the elements of concern; the overall goals which are developed from the needs assessment; specific learning outcomes or objectives which identify the exact expectations of teaching and learning in accordance with the overall goals; implementation which reflects the instructional phase; and evaluation which includes formative and summative assessment. The implementation component is critical to the overall success of a curriculum. Focus includes emphasis upon teaching styles, learning styles, teaching abilities and training, as well as learner abilities; and most eminent are the materials selected to enhance the teaching/learning process. The importance of relevant and responsive selection of materials for a multicultural environment cannot be overemphasized.

---

[1]For the purpose of this chapter, the term multicultural not only refers to racial groups, but is inclusive of linguistic, financial, environmental, physical ability, age, and sexual differences.

Traditionally, all school materials have been white, elite, and male-oriented--not reflecting the pluralistic world in which we live. Little or no focus was given to the racially different and/or females of this world. Minorities and females rarely were main characters in textbook stories, instead they were dictated to, saved, and/or led by a white male who was adventurous and daring, and who provided the answers with a happy ending. Rarely did the stories focus on women who worked; those few women who did work were portrayed either as teachers or nurses. All "good" mothers stayed at home with the children and cooked nourishingly big meals.

During the sixties, publishers and material developers began to paint textbook characters black and brown in response to the pressures of ethnic interest groups. However, little if anything was done to change the written text. The newly black and brown faces still used the same language as well as dressed and acted just like the original white, male characters. With additional pressure, textbook writers began to change the names of various characters--John became Juan and Jane became Juanita. The life styles of their characters, nevertheless, remained the same. All lived in a nice house with a white picket fence and had a father who carried a briefcase and wore a suit, white shirt, and tie to work. The mother usually stayed home while the children all went to school, had lots of friends and a grandmother who came to visit from some far off place. What a contrast to the families of today, as well as, to the culturally diverse styles of life today!

Surprisingly enough, many of the same traditional images are characteristic of the books and materials used today in upper grades and high schools. The appearance of women and identifiable racial minorities becomes less frequent as the materials and texts increase in grade level. Even more exasperating are the college-level texts which are nearly all white and male-oriented, including educational methods tests.

In addition to the images projected by traditionally used materials and texts, other media sources (e.g., television, radio, newspapers, comics) also promote negative or nonexistent images of women and minorities. The handicapped, the poor and the rich, older individuals, foreigners, and linguistically different persons are also consistently excluded from the majority of educational materials and media productions.

What does all of this mean to the classroom teacher who must select materials? What should publishers do to change the images? First, it is quite unrealistic to believe that all books and materials that do not give accurate accounts of our pluralistic society should be tossed away and forgotten. Nearly all materials have some bias and many of them are valuable for other kinds of information. All publishers, instead, should take a more aware approach in the selection of new materials for print, and all teachers should utilize the best materials available while calling students' attention to the misrepresentations.

A teacher could, for example, initiate a classroom discussion concerning the images of Indians found in most printed and media materials. The teacher might begin a discussion by asking students how many of them know what an Indian looks like? This introduction should be followed with an exploration of what is seen on television and in books in comparison to the actual individuality of each Native American tribe and the fact that in the twentieth century, the American Indian often dresses just as many others in the United States. Native American children attend school, do homework, have pets and responsibilities, and dream for an exciting future just as other children do. The unique difference occurs in the family traditions and beliefs, but everyone holds some traditions and beliefs.

When the opportunity is given to select
materials and texts, the selection process should
include a number of factors. Concern should focus
not only on the cost and durability but also on
the accuracy of contents and the positive representation of minorities, women, the handicapped,
the aged, the linguistically different, as well
as the rich and the poor. Teachers should carefully consider the images of each of the characters presented and ask if a variety of heroes and
heroines is shown. Are women portrayed as successful when presented in nontraditional roles? Are
the images presented those which would provide
positive role models for the diverse child as
well as provide meaningful exposure and new
experience for the dominant-culture child? Is
the history of all peoples accurately told or is
it given from the viewpoint of only one group?

Additional attention should be placed on the
vocabulary used in the materials and texts under
consideration. Are characters referred to as
lazy, savage, evil, or sly? Do terms denote a
negative entity? The English language, generally
the language of the texts, is often biased and
prejudiced. Many words used in connection with
race and ethnicity also express racist and negative meanings--e.g., "black as sin," "blackwash,"
"greasy" (greaser), "spik," or "branded." Often,
the phrasing suggests that the non-White individual
should change or could succeed if s/he had studied
or worked harder, spoke English better, didn't
have an accent, or wasn't so dark.

The reality of the world about us reveals a
multitude of variations within all cultural
groups. Failing to portray the diversity in life
is failing to share the truth with students.

The selection of materials should also focus
on the illustrations used and their accuracy. In
an effort to include a representation of all
racial groups, illustrators have "unconsciously"
developed stereotype characteristics for a number

of ethnic and racial groups. The Native American
is generally portrayed wearing a headdress with
war paint while the Asian American is shown as
having buck teeth and slanted lines for eyes. The
speech patterns of these textbook characters is
nearly always of a nonstandard English form,
usually indicating a halting rate. Blacks are
stereotypically represented as poor, uneducated,
and grinning individuals while the Hispanic char-
acter is illustrated as a peasant wearing a sarape
with a large sombrero.

Such illustrations not only are stereotypic
but also promote the belief that all of a particular group (e.g., Hispanics, Native Americans,
Nebraskans) are the same. This excludes the
factor, even the thought, that Native Americans
may be of the Crow, Sioux, Navajo, Cherokee, or
some other tribe. They may live in an urban
setting or on a reservation. As one focuses on
specific individual cases, the person in question
may have grown up in an adoptive family in a
uniquely different cultural experience. The
Indian child who sees pictures of so-called Indians wearing headdress and warpaint might also
become confused, believing the given image is
what is expected of him/her. The selective teacher will guard against such misconceptions.

Each illustration leads the inexperienced
onlooker to believe that this is the norm as
opposed to merely a means of depicting difference.
The child tends to take all at face value especially when s/he is not questioned about the reality.
What a shame not to know that the setting, which
may be rural or urban, middle class, coastal or
mountainous, affects the living styles of all its
peoples regardless of ethnicity. Such awareness
can be shared with students through the selective
use of culturally responsive materials.

The multiculturally aware observer should
also take into consideration the overall viewpoint
of material writers and publishers. The date of

publication can serve as a clue. One cannot
assume, just because materials are advertised as
being culturally accurate and relevant, that in
all respects they are. Because history tends to
be written by the dominant culture, one might find
inaccuracies. This is not necessarily intentional
but is often the result of interpretation and/or
point of view. By using a number of material
sources, the conscientious teacher can provide a
wide variety of viewpoints that assist in broad-
ening the experiences of the learner.

The emphasis on the selection of culturally
relevant and responsive materials and texts should
not be interpreted as meaning that the quality of
instruction and learning is to be second place to
that of cultural relevance. The fact is, however,
that learning will be enhanced by utilizing culturally responsive materials. All students will
experience accuracies, illustrations, language,
and attitudes that mirror the society surrounding
them and that include all of them as relevant
beings in that society. Through such exposure,
a more aware and feeling group of better educated
individuals will emerge.

SUMMARY

Careful selection of materials and instructional media is of great concern in the educational setting. The materials used will help to
promote the positive effect of responsive education, education that is multicultural.

REFERENCES

Committee on Sexism and Reading of the International Reading Association. "Guide for Evaluating Sex Stereotyping in Reading Materials." The Reading Teacher, 31, 3, (December 1970), 288-289.

Ethnic Heritage Studies Materials Analysis Instrument. Boulder, Colorado: Social Science Education Consortium, Inc., 1975.

Grant, Carl A. and Gloria W. Grant. "Instructional Materials in Multicultural Education." Multicultural Education: Commitments, Issues, and Applications. Washington, D.C.: 1977, 113-120.

Guidelines for Selecting Bias-Free Textbooks and Storybooks. New York: Council on Interracial Books for Children, 1980.

10 Quick Ways to Analyze Children's Books for Racism and Sexism. New York: Council on Interracial Books for Children, 1975.

Tiedt, Pamela L. and Iris M. Tiedt. Multicultural Teaching: A Handbook of Activities, Information, and Resources. Boston: Allyn and Bacon, 1979.

Unlearning "Indian" Stereotypes: A Teaching Unit for Elementary Teachers and Children's Librarians. New York: The Racism and Sexism Resource Center for Educators, 1977.

PART IV

MULTICULTURAL LESSON AND DISSEMINATION PLANS

CHAPTER 10

MULTICULTURAL LESSON AND DISSEMINATION PLANS

It is important to understand that multicultural education does not mean setting aside time from other classroom activities to study ethnic minorities. Multicultural education is centered on the premise that <u>all</u> educational subjects can and should be taught from a multicultural standpoint. References and considerations to all the varied cultures represented in a teacher's classroom and the surrounding community should be incorporated into the mathematical exercises as well as the social studies discussion.

The lesson plans included in this chapter were developed by teacher participants in the Seminar on Multiethnic Relations presented by Colorado State University faculty members in 1979 and 1980. The participating teachers were asked to identify the next unit of work they were preparing for their class and to rewrite that unit using a multiethnic/multicultural approach.

Dissemination plans were also developed by seminar participants in order to share their multicultural awareness with others.

An essential goal of the Seminar in Multiethnic Relations was to train teams of teachers to understand and to appreciate the pluralistic nature of American education. The seminar had a built-in multiplicative consequence: all participants increased their own knowledge of groups in society that are culturally different, and they learned how to offer similar awareness training for others. Participants can now employ new strategies and materials for the teacher-learner setting; this includes formulating models for incorporating multicultural content into existing curricula and for disseminating information to others.

LESSON PLANS DEVELOPED IN EDUCATION 692C

SEMINAR IN MULTIETHNIC RELATIONS

William E. Sims and Bernice Bass de Martínez

The following two lesson plans were developed
by the directors of the seminar to help stimulate
the thinking of the participants.

FIRST LEVEL LESSON PLAN

Topic: The Meaning of Ethnicity

Overview:

Students have various definitions of the
concept "ethnic group." They are aware that their
definitions are cloudy and they want to bring them
into sharper focus. It may be assumed that for
most students of today the meaning of ethnic group
could be a problem as they attempt to relate to
people in their school who are different. Throughout this plan the instructor is designated as
"teacher" and each participating student as
"student."

Specific Objectives:

To encourage small group membership, to reduce
threat and promote open-mindedness.

To arrive at a definition of ethnic group; to
understand and appreciate the social and economic
evolution of selected ethnic groups; to initiate
simple research; to increase the knowledge of the
students in the class.

174

<u>Time Required</u>:

Two class meetings.

First Class Meeting

<u>Instructional Procedures</u>:

<u>Teacher</u> - America is a nation of immigrants or descendants of immigrants; there is only one group of people that are true natives of this country. What does the term "ethnic group" mean to most of you? Let me start the discussion by naming some of the ethnic groups in America: there are Native Americans, Mexican Americans, Black Americans, German Americans, English Americans, Irish Americans, Scandinavians, Italians, Jews, Polish, Russians, Puerto Ricans, Cubans, Japanese, Chinese, Philipinos, and others that we will not name in the interest of time. The class will be given six minutes for brainstorming on ethnic groups. I will divide you into groups, "6 x 6" (six students in a group for six minutes).

At the end of the small group discussion the teacher should repeat the question: What does ethnic group mean to you?

<u>Student</u> - To me, ethnic group means a group of people who are culturally different.

<u>Student</u> - I am not sure that I understand what an ethnic group is, I just don't know.

<u>Teacher</u> - It may be worthwhile for us to see how other people have defined ethnic group. During your study period today I want you to find one article, story or book on the subject of ethnicity or ethnic group. Each person in the class should be prepared to give us some information on ethnic group(s) when you return to class.

175

Second Class Meeting

Instructional Procedures:

   Teacher - Please share with the class the
ideas you have gained from your reading. I will
list your ideas on the blackboard. After an
appropriate length of time and an adequate list
of ideas, I want you to return to the small group
you were in yesterday. From each group I want a
short paragraph defining an ethnic group. You
may use any of the ideas listed on the board, and
you may change them to fit the wishes of the group.

   Each group work can continue for ten minutes.

   Teacher - Now we need to divide the ethnic
groups into what we shall call white ethnics and
minority ethnics. What groups would you list under
white ethnics? (Teacher should place two categories on the board.)

   Student - Under white ethnics I would place
Swedes and Poles.

   Teacher - That is correct. What about some
others?

   Student - I believe German and Irish should
also be placed under the heading of white ethnics.

   After a reasonable number have been listed
the teacher can ask students to list minority
ethnics.

   The following definitions should be dittoed
and distributed to the class:

   White Ethnics: A human Caucasian collectivity
that has immigrated to this country and that has
retained a common and distinctive culture within
enclaves in major cities and rural communities.
White ethnics are identified as: Swedes, Poles,
German, Irish, Italian, Danes, Norwegians, Czechs,

176

Egyptian, Syrian, Lebanese.

   Minority Ethnics: A human non-Caucasian
collectivity that has immigrated to this country
and that has retained a common and distinctive
culture within enclaves in major cities and rural
communities. Minority ethnics are identified as:
American Indians, Blacks, Chicanos, Chinese,
Japanese, Mexican Americans, Puerto Ricans, and
Vietnamese.

   Conduct a discussion of concepts and generalizations in order to discover what each student
has learned from the lessons.

                SECOND LEVEL LESSON PLAN

   As educators, subtle things we do promote
either cultural awareness and acceptance, or
cultural prejudices. The manner in which our
lessons are presented, the materials we use, and
the comments we make all influence (promote)
awareness or prejudice.

   FOR EXAMPLE:

   1. Do we analyze other language (dialect)
       patterns to help youngsters realize
       that each has a structure?

   2. Do we include the listings of contribu-
       tions of other significant ethnic
       figures when teaching history?

   3. Do we discuss the nutritional value of
       ethnic foods when we present nutritional
       units in home economics?

   4. Do we utilize cultural names positively

                        177

when we are writing story problems for
math?

5. Do we teach the games and dances of visi-
    ble minority groups when we present units
    on dance and folkways?

6. Do we provide opportunities for ethnical-
    ly different students to interact and
    work together?

7. Do we consciously measure and choose our
    words to eliminate terminology that is
    biased and that carries racial overtones?

8. Do we consider the historical impact of
    culturally different peoples?

9. Do we analyze the herbs and medicinal
    cures utilized by the "others" in our
    school community when presenting general
    health and living units?

10. Do we include visuals of ethnically
    different students actively involved
    in learning?

This list can be endless. If we, as teachers,
become aware of the effects of our actions, attitudes, and behaviors, we can make our teaching
responsive to a multiethnic and culturally pluralistic environment.

The lesson plan that you develop for second
level planning is one that will directly reflect
your subject matter and teaching assignment. To
prepare this plan, begin by identifying the next
unit of work to be prepared for presentation to
your class, then recall the experiences and readings developed during your participation in this
seminar.

Now, rewrite your next unit of work and
incorporate as many multicultural aspects/elements

178

as possible.   This revised unit will be your
second level lesson plan.

LESSON PLAN

by

Glen Berry

Topic: <u>Study of Sets</u>

<u>Specific Objectives</u>:

For the student to:

1. Apply sets and theory to cultural and
    ethnic grouping of people as members of
    a set.

2. Understand how cultural groups inter-
    relate as members of a set and subsets
    (subculture).

<u>Entrance Skills</u>:

The student must have some knowledge of his
own cultural background. The student must have
basic knowledge of sets and subsets.

<u>Materials Needed</u>:

Pencil, paper, pictures of people of White,
Black, and Hispanic origin, chalk board.

<u>Time Required</u>:

One hour.

<u>Instructional Procedures</u>:

1. Make a list of the 12 most predominant
    races of people (greatest number) in
    America (e.g., Native American, German,
    Irish). Write them on the chalk board.
    This is a universal set.

180

2. Have students make a set of all races
    that are {White}, {Black}, {Hispanic}.

3. Make a set {   } of all physical charac-
    teristics that all races have in common,
    such as hands, feet, skin, etc.

4. Make a set {   } of characteristics that
    differentiate people--such as color,
    religion, sex, culture, etc.

5. Make a set {of all White races} union (U)
    with a set {of all Black races} in the
    universal set.

6. Make a subset as follows:
    {races in the universal set} ⊂ {Hispanic}

Evaluation:

1. Have the students actually form into
    groups to illustrate which set they
    belong to such as the set of Whites,
    Hispanics, and Blacks.

2. Have the students actually form into a
    universal group to illustrate the common
    characteristics.

3. Have the students form into subsets ⊂ of
    the Hispanic set.

4. Re-form the entire group to show they all
    belong to the universal set of American
    culture.

LESSON PLAN

by

Karen Lewis

Topic: Denver, A Center of Expansion and Change

Specific Objectives:

1. Students will discuss which ethnic
    groups' contributions have influenced
    the development of Denver.

2. Students will discuss how ethnic tradi-
    tions have become a part of urban life.

3. Students will be more aware of ethnic
    agencies in Denver and the type(s) of
    assistance offered.

4. Students will be more aware of ethnic
    places, names, and landmarks in Denver.

Entrance Skills:

    Students will have participated in a group
activity concerning what constitutes an ethnic
group and a discussion relative to the characteristics of ethnic group identity.

Materials Needed:

1. Research materials: Encyclopedias,
    texts, magazines, articles

2. A listing of various agencies with
    information relating to ethnic group
    activities in the Denver area

    a. B'nai B'rith

    b. Social Science Consortium

182

c. Cultural Heritage Center

d. Adams County Historic Society

e. Denver area ethnic clubs

f. Denver Public Library

Time Required:

Three to four class periods.

Instructional Procedures:

Discuss with the students:

1. What traditions did ethnic groups bring to Denver? And where did these traditions come from?

2. How do the traditions of various ethnic groups become a part of urban living?

3. Why is it important that different ethnic groups keep some of the customs of their native land?

4. Does sharing ethnic customs and traditions bring people closer together? If so, how? If not, why not?

5. How can people learn more about the customs, values and traditions of various ethnic groups?

6. Which landmarks, parks, agencies, streets, etc., in Denver are named after persons belonging to various ethnic groups?

7. Which ethnic groups were responsible for the early development of Denver? And, what did these groups contribute to its development as a city?

183

Student Activities:

One ethnic group to be selected by each team; students will divide into teams of three to complete the following:

1. Students will investigate the early development of Denver relative to the various ethnic groups which have contributed to its development.

2. Students will visit and/or contact B'nai B'rith, the state Cultural Heritage Center, and local historic agencies to gather information with regard to various ethnic groups that have had a part in the development of Denver.

3. Students will compile reports relating the information they have gathered. Reports will be shared through group presentations to the class.

4. Large group and small group discussions will be held to discuss student findings. Teacher-directed discussion questions will be used to tie all student information together with regard to the topic of ethnicity and its relationship to urban living.

Evaluation:

Students will be evaluated through the following procedures:

1. Written reports

2. Group presentations

3. Large and small group discussions

LESSON PLAN

by

Karen Lewis

Topic: Ethnic Logos

Specific Objectives:

1. Students will discuss the use of
    symbolic logos by various businesses,
    social organizations and interest
    groups.

2. Students will discuss the psychological
    determination involved in the selection
    of advertising logos.

3. Students will increase their awareness
    of their own psychological view of
    symbols through the creation of their
    own logos.

Entrance Skills:

    Students will have researched the ethnicity
and representation of ethnic groups in the local
community and the Denver metropolitan area and
will be aware of the types of agencies and social
organizations of these groups.

Materials Needed:

1. Drafting supplies, printing materials

2. Cameras

3. Tag or poster board

Time Required:

    Four to five class periods

Instructional Procedures:

1. Have the students research the use of graphic symbols as identifying signs for persons, companies, and interest groups in the community.

2. Students will discuss psychological group needs that are met by symbols and the positive and negative effects they may have on other groups or persons.

3. Students will bring in symbols they have found to be used in the community and discuss their intended and possible hidden messages.

4. Students will discuss symbols as they relate to their personal identity and values.

Student Activities:

1. Following the research of symbols in the local community, students will divide into groups of three or four students to develop a logo for a selected organization:

   a. A Black-owned and operated manufacturing company

   b. A feminist legal counseling firm

   c. A Hispanic political party

   d. An ethnic employment agency

2. Students will share and discuss their logos as to how and why they were developed.

3. Students will participate in a discussion of:

a. What psychological factors influenced their selection of a logo?

b. What population(s) were they trying to influence through their logos?

c. How adequately do the logos represent the portrayed agency? Is the image positive or negative?

d. How do the student-developed logos compare to logos evidenced in the local community?

Evaluation:

Students will be evaluated through the following procedures:

1. Large and small group discussions.

2. Small group cooperation and effort.

3. Final student-developed logos and class presentation.

DISSEMINATION PLANS DEVELOPED IN EDUCATION 692C

SEMINAR IN MULTIETHNIC RELATIONS

The following outline was developed by the directors of the seminar to assist participants in building their own dissemination plans.

THE DISSEMINATION PLAN

by

William E. Sims and Bernice Bass de Martínez

General Information:

The final objective of this course is to make the experience and expertise that each of you have developed available to others. This is to be done through the development and implementation of "sharing" or a dissemination plan.

Procedure:

1. Work as a team (the team should be composed of course participants from the same school).

2. Identify the target audience for your plan (who will receive the benefits of your presentations and the sharing).

3. Prepare a goal statement with specific objectives. For example:

   Goal: This dissemination plan is designed to make the teachers and special staff at _____ school more aware of the contributions made by ethnic minorities.

188

The goal of this plan is
to make all building
staff cognizant of the
behaviors which might
create cultural conflict.

The purpose of this plan
is to help teachers
become aware of the
unique differences
between education that
is multicultural and
education in general.

Objective: a. To produce a news-
letter on a monthly
basis that will
include contributions
of visible minorities.

b. To hold regular multi-
ethnic discussion
sessions with all
building staff.

c. To have the staff
analyze their inter-
actions with cultural-
ly different students.

d. To help teachers
eliminate cross-
cultural conflict
through the develop-
ment of different
styles.

4. Describe how you will implement your plan
and exactly what will be done and when.

<u>Other Information</u>:

1. This plan should be implemented during this school year.

2. Two copies of the plan should be submitted for reading and review by the course facilitators the last class meeting. Include all team member names. Those wishing to receive the returned plan should include an address for mailing.

DISSEMINATION PLAN

by

Barbara N. Allen and Shirley Bunch

Target Audience:

West and East Middle Schools, Aurora Public Schools, Aurora, Colorado.

Goal:

This dissemination plan is designed to make the teachers and special staffs at West and East Middle Schools more aware of the ethnic and cultural differences and contributions made by the Asian American and Black ethnic minorities.

Objectives:

1. To promote an awareness of multicultural and multiethnic differences.

2. To provide a variety of multiethnic activities and strategies that teachers might be able to implement in their classes.

Methods of Implementation:

To arrange through school district funds to have Dr. Siri Vongthieres from the Colorado Department of Education and Dr. Jennie Green, Multicultural Consultant, to present a half-day inservice to both schools on the first inservice day of the school year. The audience will be divided into two groups with Siri and Jennie doing their presentations to each group separately. (Then the groups will rotate.)

191

DISSEMINATION PLAN

by

Marjorie Schmitz and Lynn Morris

Target Audience:

Teachers at Clayton School.

Objectives:

We have a period set aside each day (35 minutes) for values discussion and multicultural/
multiethnic education. Teachers seldom use this
time for m/m education. On the basis of the
situation, our objectives are the following:

1. To raise the involvement level of our
   staff in regard to multicultural/multi-
   ethnic education.

2. To raise the sensitivity level of our
   staff in regard to the needs of minority
   students.

Methods of Implementation:

1. Invite a speaker to speak to the staff
   about life/values/problems of a minority
   group in the U.S.

2. Set up ethnic games for use in classroom,
   playground and media center. (We're
   going to try to discuss the effectiveness
   of these games on an informal basis with
   the teachers.)

3. Create a hall bulletin board displaying
   achievements of minority persons.

4. Place materials in faculty lounge concern-
   m/m lessons. (We'll first briefly talk
   about these materials in a faculty

meeting.)

Time Schedule:

     1st quarter - methods 3 and 4

     2nd quarter - method 1

     3rd quarter - method 2

DISSEMINATION PLAN
by
Marjorie Schmitz and Lynn Morris

Target Audience:

     District I Music Teachers

Goal:

     Lynn Morris will be teaching an inservice to all district music teachers and will incorporate the following goal into her sessions:

     To help music teachers become more aware of the benefits of m/m education in daily music classes.

Methods of Implementation:

    1. Provide guidance for music teachers in developing lesson plans for their particular school setting.

    2. Music teachers will complete a lesson plan, use it in their classes, and share the results with the group.

Time Schedule:

     1st quarter - methods 1 and 2

DISSEMINATION PLAN

by

Louise Draeger

Target Audience:

This dissemination plan is designed to make the teachers and students of Alsup School, Commerce City, more aware of the musical contributions made by ethnic minorities.

Objectives:

As a music teacher, I chose to explore the field of music to discover the ethnic backgrounds of pertinent musicians. My intention is to compile this list of musicians by ethnic groups so that it can be used by teachers and students alike. The final product might serve as a means for improving the self-concept of certain minority students; it might supply new information to teachers and students; and it might serve as a source of inspiration for future bulletin boards, study projects, bibliographic sketches, or reports.

Methods of Implementation:

In researching this project, I looked into all aspects of music: classical, rock, country, performance, composition, conducting, blues, jazz, dance, arranging . . . and any other related subject. The ethnic groups I studied are divided into five major categories: Anglo American, Mexican American, Asian American, Black American, and Native American. While it might seem strange to include Anglo American in a list of contributions made by ethnic minorities in the field of music, I feel that the Anglo American contribution cannot be forgotten.

194

<u>Results</u>:

I found this study most interesting. The results were not quite what I had expected. Bear in mind that this is an on-going project. It is far from finished as there are many, many names I have not yet added to the list. This is only a start.

NATIVE AMERICAN

Buffy St. Marie   Folksinger, often sings of Indian struggles.

Cher Bono   Singer, entertainer.

Joan Baez   Singer, also listed in Mexican American listing. Born Staten Island, New York, 1941. Folk songs about peace, war resistance, social ills such as farm workers' movement.

MEXICAN AMERICAN

Joan Baez   Folksinger, also listed as a Native American. Born in Staten Island, New York, 1941. Her topics for songs include peace, war resistance, and social causes such as the farm workers' movement.

Trini Lopez   Singer, entertainer.

Vikki Carr   Chicana entertainer from Los Angeles.

Born in El Paso, Texas
and named Florencia
Bisenta de Casillas
Martínez Cardona.
Named "Singer of the
Year" by the American
Guild of Variety
Artists, 1972. Start-
ed the Vikki Carr
Scholarship Foundation
to assist Mexican
Americans in further-
ing their education.

Freddy Fender

Popular country singer.

Linda Ronstadt

I still question this.
Found her name on a
list of Mexican Ameri-
can entertainers.
Have yet to verify this
information. Singer,
born in Tucson,
Arizona.

ANGLO AMERICAN

Aaron Copland

Composer/conductor, of
Russian-Jewish parents.
Received Pulitzer
Prize in 1954 for music
to "Appalacian Spring,"
a ballet. Other impor-
tant compositions
include "Rodeo," "Billy
the Kid," and "The Red
Pony Suite."

Dave Brubeck

One of the first class-
ically trained musi-
cians to play jazz
successfully. Born in
California, studied
with Darius Milhaud.

Important compositions
include: "Light in
the Wilderness," an
oratoria; "The Gates
of Justice," a can-
tata; "Elements," a
work for jazz quartet
and orchestra. Most
often associated with
composition "Take
Five."

Leonard Bernstein   Composer/conductor, of
                       Jewish American back-
                       ground. Became con-
                       ductor of New York
                       Philharmonic Orchestra
                       in 1958. Writes class-
                       ical as well as popular
                       music. Most famous
                       composition "West Side
                       Story," a musical about
                       ethnic minorities in
                       New York City.

Gunther Schuller   Composer/conductor,
                       president of New
                       England Conservatory
                       of Music, Boston.
                       Combines classical and
                       jazz to create "3rd
                       stream music." Also
                       does scholarly research
                       in jazz and ragtime
                       music.

Pete Seeger   Folksinger/composer.
                       His songs are about
                       people. "If I Had a
                       Hammer," one of his
                       more popular songs.

Stephen Foster   Songwriter, of Irish
                       American parents,

	1826-1864. Real name Stephen Foster Collins. Composed Black folk songs called "plantation melodies": "Old Black Joe," "Old Folks at Home," "My Old Kentucky Home, Good Night," "Beautiful Dreamer," "Camptown Races," and "Oh Susanna." In all, Foster wrote more than 200 songs.
Woody Guthrie	Folksinger/composer. Traveled during the depression and dust bowl days composing songs about people and their plights. More popular songs include: "This Land is Your Land," "So Long, It's Been Good to Know You."
Meredith Wilson	Composer. Wrote popular musical "Music Man."
Otto Luening	Composer/conductor. A native of Milwaukee, Wisconsin, he studied flute and theory in Germany. Pioneer in avant-garde electronic music, key organizer in setting up Columbia-Princeton Electronic Music Center, 1959.
Janis Joplin	Rock singer. Born Port Arthur, Texas. Sang with Big Brother

and the Holding Company, achieved fame for blues and soul songs. 1943-1970

Van Cliburn   Pianist, from Kilgore, Texas, born 1934. Won the International Tchaikovsky Competition in Moscow, 1958. Solos with major symphony orchestras all over the world.

Barbra Streisand   Singer, born New York City, 1942. Classically trained singer, but starred on Broadway and in motion pictures. Known for roles in "Funny Girl," and "Hello Dolly."

F. M. Christianson   Composer/conductor. of Norwegian immigrant parents. Composed numerous sacred choral works, started the St. Olaf Choir, known for sacred singing and acapella performances.

Chuck Mangione   Jazz musician. From Buffalo, New York, of Italian American background. Began as trumpet player, switched to fluglehorn while studying at Eastman School of Music. Directs, writes and arranges for his own jazz band.

Elvis Presley

Rock singer. Most
outstanding white
musician in rhythm
and blues. Influenced
future white rhythm
and blues musicians.
Early name in rock-
n-roll movement of the
fifties.

Fred Waring

Conductor/arranger.
Formed the choral
group called "Fred
Waring's Pennsylvani-
ans," toured the
country giving musical
shows.

Antonia Brico

Conductor. Raised in
California, studied
in Germany as a
pianist. Was the first
woman to conduct the
Metropolitan Opera,
also formed the New
York Women's Symphony
in New York, 1933-1939.
Lives in Denver and now
conducts the Brico
Symphony.

William Revelli

Conductor. Began as a
concert violinist but
ended up as director
of the University of
Michigan bands. Over
the years as director,
he has raised band
performance standards
both as marching and
concert units. Found-
ed the College Band
Directors National
Association, 1941.

Bob Dylan	Singer/composer. Born Hibbing, Minnesota as Robert Zimmerman. Began as guitar singing protest musician. More popular songs include "Blowin' in the Wind," "Lay, Lady Lay."
Artie Shaw	Jazz musician. Born New York City, 1910. Clarinetist with outstanding technique. Billie Holiday sang with the group for a short period in a time when racial barriers existed in jazz bands.
Judy Collins	Folksinger, composer. Started in the folk protest movement to later become popular singer. Was a piano student of Antonia Brico in Denver.
Woody Herman	Band leader, clarinet-est. Born Woodrow Wilson Herman, 1913. Began in vaudeville, switched to performer/arranger with Isham Jones Orchestra.

BLACK AMERICANS

Hubert Laws	Jazz musician. Classically trained on the flute, went on to perform jazz in small group ensembles often blending jazz sounds

	with classical compositions.
J.H. & S.L. Dickinson	Invented first player piano.
Louis Armstrong	Jazz musician, trumpeter. The first internationally jazz soloist. Born New Orleans, 1900, died 1971. Started playing coronet at age of 13 in detention home. 1922 went to Chicago to join the King Oliver band. After playing with King Oliver for a few years, left to form his own group, as well as to work with other groups. First musician to sing in skat style, rhythmic nonsense syllables in place of words. Hits include "Mack, the Knife," "Hello, Dolly."
W.C. Handy	Father of blues. Hits include "St. Louis Blues" and "Beale Street Blues."
Marian Anderson	Singer. First Black to sing a leading role in the Metropolitan Opera, 1955.
Eartha Kitt	Singer/actress. Born 1928.
Joel Walker Sweeny	Perfected banjo.

Aretha Franklin	Composer, pianist, singer of gospel and soul music. Daughter of a preacher. Franklin represented the Detroit Motown sound. She was "Queen of Soul" in the late sixties. Hits include "Respect," "I Never Love a Man."
Paul Robeson	Singer/actor. Born 1926.
Jubilee Singers of Fisk University	First Black performing group to call attention to spirituals as concert material. Gave concert tours starting in 1870s.
Billie Holiday	Jazz singer, and interpreter of blues and pop songs 1915-1959. Worked with Benny Goodman. Her autobiography is a well-known book: "Lady Sings the Blues."
Mahalia Jackson	Gospel singer. Born 1911 in New Orleans. Trained as a gospel singer at church where her father was minister. Later moved to Chicago where she began her singing career. Known foremost as a gospel singer with a slight jazz influence.
Chuck Berry	Singer, composer, guitarist. Born 1926

in St. Louis. Was a
big hit in early rock
years with songs like
"Maybellene" and
"Sweet Little Sixteen."
Popularity declined in
late fifties, but
reappeared in late
sixties with "My
Ding-a-Ling." Was
an influence for the
Beatles and Rolling
Stones.

James Brown

Singer. Soul singer
in sixties, first big
hit "Out of Sight."
Also "Papa's Got a
Brand New Bag." Brown
also included "black
pride" songs such as
"Say It Loud, I'm
Black and I'm Proud,"
which was a landmark
for Blacks.

Leontyne Price

Opera singer. Soprano
with classical back-
ground. Born in Massa-
chusetts, and studied
at the Julliard School
of Music in New York.
Has starred in "Porgy
and Bess," "Aida,"
and Il Trovatore."

Stevie Wonder

Singer, composer,
musician. Rhythm and
blues musician of the
sixties. Born 1950,
Saginaw, Michigan as
Stevland Morris. Has
been blind all his
life. Hits include:

"You Are the Sunshine
of My Life," "Super-
stition," and "Higher
Ground."

Ethel Waters

Singer and actress of
American stage and
screen. 1896-1977.

Fats Waller

Pianist, composer,
organist. Born Thomas
Wright Waller in New
York City, 1904.
Father a minister, so
grew up in church tradi-
tion of organ playing,
switched to piano, and
jazz. Hits include:
"Honeysuckle Rose"
and "Ain't Misbehavin'."

Libba Cotten

Singer, composer. Hits
include: "Freight
Train," "Here Rattler,"
"Washington Blues."

Eubie Blake

Pianist, composer.
Popular in ragtime era.
Began career in Balti-
more night clubs.
Composed "Charleston
Rag" in 1898. Broadway
musical entitled "Eubie"
is about Eubie Blake.

Alberta Hunter

Singer. Ran away from
home at age 11 to sing
in Chicago. Wrote
"Downhearted Blues"
which became a hit.
Worked in New York City
under the name of
Josephine Beatty.
Toured with the USO

during WW II.

Earl Hines

Jazz pianist. Often known as "Fatha" Hines. Was a pioneer of solo jazz piano in a time when jazz piano players were simply playing harmony and chords.

Harry Belafonte

Singer, composer, guitarist. Born in New York City, 1927. Lived in Jamaica from age 8-13. Known for his dramatic interpretations of folk songs.

Bessie Smith

Jazz singer. Interpreter of blues. Born in Chattanooga, Tennessee in 1890s. Early training was in church singing, went on to become a hit, singing blues with jazz greats such as Fletcher Henderson, Coleman Hawkins, and Benny Goodman. Career cut short in 1938 when she was killed in a car accident.

James Weldon Johnson

Composer of "Lift Every Voice and Sing."

John Coltrane

Jazz saxophone player. First recognition came as tenor saxophone player. In later years rediscovered the soprano saxophone. Interpreter of modern jazz, often displayed a violent style of playing. Was one of first musicians to reflect music of India. Was also known as a composer. One of his finest works is the album "My Favorite Things" and "Love Supreme."

| Ann Hobson | Harpist. Associate principal harpist with the Boston Symphony Orchestra, and principal harpist with the Boston Pops Orchestra. Grew up and was musically trained in Philadelphia. |

| Duke Ellington | Jazz leader. Born Edward Kennedy in Washington D.C., 1899. Leader of Duke Ellington Orchestra, achieved early fame in Harlem in 1920s. Has played all over the world, composed numerous works, both jazz and classical, and concertized at Carnegie Hall. |

| Alvin Ailey American Dance Theater | Black dance group first formed in 1960s and still popular as contemporary dance group. |

| Charlie Parker | Jazz musician. Born in Kansas City, 1920, grew up playing saxophone in blues |

tradition. Nick-
named "Bird," or
Hardbird." Displayed
much technique on his
saxophone, responsible
for birth of bebop
sound in jazz.

Scott Joplin

Ragtime composer,
pianist. Son of a
former slave born in
Texarkana, Texas, 1968.
Left home at 14 and
played in Mississippi
Valley bars. Settled
in Sedalia, Missouri.
In all, wrote 500
works including a
ballet and 2 operas.
Went on to New York
to dind a producer
for his stage works,
but died in the
process. Hits include:
"Easy Winners," "Maple
Leaf Rag." Died 1919.

Ma Rainey

Blues singer. Born
Gertrude Malissa
Pridgett, Columbus,
Ohio in 1886. Started
with minstrel shows and
other various travel-
ing shows and circus
acts. Her blues style
was a direct influence
for Bessie Smith.

Dizzy Gillespie

Jazz musician. Born
John Birks Gillespie
in 1917. Trumpet
player. Early in
career got name Dizzy

	for his clowning around.
Ella Fitzgerald	Jazz singer. Born 1918, Newport News, Virginia. Her first big hit was "A Tisket, A Tasket" in 1938. Went on to record with many big jazz stars.
Miles Davis	Jazz trumpeter. Grew up in East St. Louis. Had some formal training at Julliard School of Music, but favored jazz instead of classical music. Began working with jazz stars while in New York, toured with a number of big name groups, and finally formed his own group.
Count Basie	Pianist. Born William Basie in Red Bank, New Jersey in early 1900s. Acquired music fundamentals from Fats Waller and other New York jazz musicians. Popular in the 1930s swing era.

AFTERWORD

School personnel are now expected to understand the complex role of ethnicity in American education, yet most of the teachers and other school staff trained in past years were not exposed to the information needed to cope with today's multicultural populations, particularly those in our schools. The overall purpose of this work was to provide insights for the practicing teacher as well as for s/he who is preparing to teach. The organization of the book focused on those areas which in the opinion of the authors provide the better mode of helping teachers broaden their knowledge base and understanding.

The first sections focused on the legal and historical aspects affecting minorities while the next section explored the literature and folklore of visible ethnic groups. Information regarding the evaluation of and assistance to multiethnic and multiculturally impacted settings was also incorporated. The last sections promoted concrete ideas and models that might be implemented as a means of changing classroom environments to better serve minority students, including effective selection and use of responsive materials and teaching behaviors which promote positive learning and the elimination of cultural conflicts.

Through this text, not only can teachers and other school personnel receive further information, but hopefully, all students will benefit from the awakening awarenesses developed by the readers ... if this occurs, then we as authors can be called facilitators and we have accomplished our goal.

ABOUT THE AUTHORS

William E. Sims is a professor in the Department of Education at Colorado State University, Fort Collins. He is a former dean and president of Langston University. He has served as a consultant for higher education institutions throughout the United States. Dr. Sims was awarded the M.A. and Ed.D. degrees by the University of Northern Colorado. He is a member of Phi Delta Kappa, Association for the Study of Negro Life and History, Association for Supervision and Curriculum Development, Colorado Personnel and Guidance Association, and the Editorial Board of the Western Journal for "Black Studies." Dr. Sims has written for journals and has authored or contributed to four different books.

Dr. Bernice Bass de Martínez served as the Associate Director of the Ethnic Heritage Project at Colorado State University. Her other duties at the University include work in the Reading Unit and in the Teacher Education Program for undergraduates. Additionally, Dr. Martínez is involved with local, state, and national efforts in support of bilingual multicultural education. She previously taught at New Mexico Highlands University and served as a Curriculum and Instructional Materials Specialist to a Rural Educational Development Project in Cochabamba, BOLIVIA before coming to Colorado State University.

Her doctorate was earned in Curriculum and Instruction with emphasis in bilingual education, reading and language arts, and teacher training at the University of Florida, Gainesville. Other degrees were earned at the University of Northern Colorado in Greeley. Dr. Martínez is an active member of a number of organizations including the National Association of Bilingual Education, the International Reading Association, and Pi Lambda Theta.

She has written many articles related to multicultural and bilingual education and serves as a consultant for educational programs for the "traditionally underrepresented" nationally.